# Get Up Off Your Butt
# & Do It NOW!

To Say,

Thanks for helping me out about 7 years ago when I 1st started speaking. I respect your authenticity and your gregarious personality.

We may not talk much, but you have a special place in my heart and I appreciat the personal & professional friendship that we started.

Continue to bless the world with your gifts.

JERMAINE

# Get Up Off Your Butt &

# Do It NOW!

## Staying Motivated
## Even When You Don't Feel Like It

# JERMAINE M. DAVIS

*Success is a choice!*

*Expert Publishing, Inc.*
*Andover, Minnesota*

ISBN 1-931945-19-5

Library of Congress Catalog Number: 2004109442

Printed in the United States of America

First Printing: August 2004

08  07  06  05  04     5  4  3  2  1

Expert Publishing, Inc.
14314 Thrush Street NW
Andover, MN 55304-3330
1-877-755-4966
*www.expertpublishinginc.com*

## Gregory "LiL Yeat" Davis

I miss you so, so much. I miss you more than anyone will ever really know. When you departed mother Earth a part of me definitely departed with you. I will forever cry internally when I think of you. The thing I miss the most is the smile you would have on your face when I would walk through the kitchen door. I promise I will continue to make it happen in life and pursue my dreams and goals as you always encouraged me to do. I remember the last conversation we shared on my birthday over the telephone when you told me to, "just keep doing what you're doing until you blow up big and make it happen, J.D." I will always remember those words with every speech I give and every book I write. Thank you, for allowing me to love you, meet you, and experience you. I will love you forever, peace!

Thank you for sharing your life with me between 1981-2003.

### *Carolyn Charmaine Davis*

We did it, Ma! I did it, Ma! I told you that I would make you proud of me one day. When people read this book they will be reading all the jewels, precious pearls, and words of wisdom you gave to me on my journey of becoming a man. I know you're not in the best of health presently, but you will forever live through my speeches, writings, and teachings. I promise you will not be forgotten—you will live through me.

You are the #1 WOMAN in my life. Love your son, J.D.!

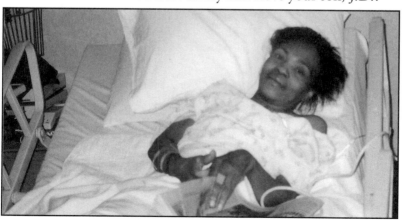

# Table of Contents

## Part 4: The Eight Steps to Making Success Happen

# Acknowledgments

Wow! There are so many people I need to thank and acknowledge personally and professionally. First, I would like to thank the Creator for placing me in situations where I realized that I had to share my gifts and talents with the present world and future generations. I thank the Creator for constantly giving me signs and signals that I must write this book even when I did not feel like it. Thank you, Creator, for giving me the tools to write this book.

A special thanks to the leading lady in my life, my mother, Carolyn Charmaine Davis. We did not have financial riches and material things growing up, but you gave me something more valuable; you gave me hope, guidance, encouragement, and values to live by. You taught me to be clean, smart, independent, and self-sufficient.

To my Uncle Ricky, who always told me, "JD, you gotta shuffle your feet and try to make a beat." You always taught me to make things happen and not to wait and depend on others.

To my brother R. Andrae' Dobbey, thanks for being a true big brother and a friend. Thanks for challenging my ideas and putting me in my place when I needed it most. We're going to make it, Drae'; I remember all those late night talks.

To my grandmother, "The Old Girl," Margaret Ann Davis, thanks for all the heart-to-heart talks even when we bumped heads. You always told me after every conversation, "Don't complain because complaining won't change your situation, and I'm proud of you, Grandson."

To my little sister Katrina, I know it's rough for you right now, and remember no matter what, I still love you. Thanks for all the fun times of laughing, dancing, and taking pictures when I came home to visit.

Lil' Greg (Lil' Yeat), my little brother, I miss you so, so much; I am crying as I write this sentence. Thank you for giving me the twenty-one years that you gave me. You have etched an indelible mark inside of me for an eternity.

To my uncles, Michael "Dinky" Davis and Kenny Davis, thanks for teaching me how to survive on the streets at an early age. I would not be who I am today without the guidance from the leaders and members of The Way of Holiness Mission in Chicago, Illinois. Thank you for trusting and investing in me. I will never ever forget all the life lessons that I learned when I was a part of your organization.

Thank you, Davia S. Hickman, for showing me greatness and friendship when I was attending Elmhurst College.

To my best friend of over 25 years, Tumchee Howard, thanks for being there through many ups and downs. You were there when we were so broke that all we could afford to eat was Ramen Noodles, ten packs for a $1.00, that we purchased at Walgreen's. I believe in you, Man. Don't stop! I love you.

To my best friend, Tanya Rieger, where do I begin? You believed in me, and you conveyed it to me since day one. You were there for my very first paid speaking engagement in June of 1997, and you were the first to ever videotape any of my presentations. Thanks for allowing me to be myself over the years. Thanks for all the intellectually stimulating discussions, and, of course, for our verbal blows.

Mwanga Williams, thanks for being the same supportive and goofy friend since high school. You inspire me to be better at what I do because you have always believed in me. You are by far my most complimentary friend.

William "Dubb-T" McCreary, you were sent to me by the Creator as a blessing in disguise. Thanks for being there throughout all my ups and downs; I really appreciate the heart-to-heart talks. Thanks for being my right hand man; I believe in you, so quit playing around, and use those God-given gifts and talents.

Herbert Grace, from the very day I met you, you pushed me to write a book. You would say, "Jermaine, you need to write a book, brother; you need to write a book." It was your voice that resonated inside my head whenever I saw you; you were my reminder. Thanks for challenging me even when I hated it; it has helped me tremendously. Thanks for coming to my presentations; you would just sit in the back of the room while I was speaking and nod your head and smile.

Terry Phillips, I know for sure that you were God sent. I did not even know you, and you believed in me. The Creator used you to uplift my spirit when I doubted myself at times. When I felt depressed, you left positive messages on my voice mail. Whenever I would get off the phone with you, I would feel like I was ready to take on the world. My favorite encouraging message that you always left for me and that I will never forget is, "You're going to make it, Jermaine. I know it. I know you're going to make it." Thanks Terry!

I would like to graciously thank Laurel Hagge for her editing gift and expertise. Thank you for being extremely efficient, effective, easy-going, and flexible. You are a true professional Laurel.

I want to thank all the teachers, counselors, and advisors who have touched my life in one way or another: Thank you for using your gifts to push the potential that I had inside of me, and thanks for taking time out to recognize my gifts and talents. I would like to personally thank all of you, starting from elementary school to graduate school: Virginia McDermott; Judy Reid; Jane Foulser; Peggy Killian; Michael Friedman, Ph.D.; Brenda Forrester, Ph.D.; Andrew Prinz, Ph.D.; and Al Katz, Ph.D.

To my alma maters, thanks for the intellectual ride at Elmhurst College and the University of Wisconsin-Superior.

Special thanks to Barbara Horvath for assisting me with this book by sharing your editing expertise. Thanks for being so fast, flexible, reliable, and upbeat. I liked your energy right from our very first meeting. You were sent as a blessing when I really needed help.

Darin Green, thank you for all the inspiration and encouragement since the birth of our professional and personal friendship. I admire your dedication to your calling, and I value your advice. Thanks for sharing your experiences with me and continuously believing in me.

# Part 1:
## The PVG Theory

## Introduction

Before I discuss the foundation of goal setting and goal achieving, I must explain one imperative concept that is essentially connected to all levels of success in life, school, & work: the **"P.V.G. Theory."**

## The P.V.G. Theory

The initials "P.V.G." stand for **Purpose, Vision, and Goals.** Each and every goal you set in life must have a purpose. Always ask yourself, "Why do I need or want to achieve this particular goal?" Having a purpose answers this question. Purpose is the reason you strive to reach each goal. Purpose tells you why you pursue certain goals and disregard others. If you do not have a valid purpose for pursuing your goal, I guarantee you will not give 100 percent to the process of goal setting and goal achieving.

## Purpose

**Ask yourself,** "What happens when we do not understand the purpose of a goal?" When we do not understand the purpose of our goals we react in one of four ways: we procrastinate, we lose sight of our dreams, we give up and quit, or we become easily distracted. When we understand the purpose for each of our goals, these distractions rarely happen. When we know the purpose of our goals, we are acknowledging the fact that we understand what is driving and directing our actions and efforts toward success.

Knowing our purpose helps us understand the compelling forces within each of us that drive our behaviors. I believe knowing and understanding your purpose will be your anchor when feelings of discouragement, depression, helplessness, and hopelessness visit you. And, believe me, they will come to visit you without a warm invitation. Discouragement, depression,

helplessness, and hopelessness have been responsible for destroying and killing millions of dreams, goals, and aspirations all
over the globe.

When we understand the purpose for each of our goals, we
can begin to visualize and develop a mental picture or image
of the specific goal we have in mind. We cannot visualize what
we do not understand. Having a mental picture of our goals
is the key to achieving them. We must be able to see what we
are pursuing in our mind. When we are unclear and uncertain
about what we are trying to accomplish, the picture or image in
our minds becomes distorted, cloudy, and fuzzy. It is extremely
difficult to pursue a goal that is ambiguous and distorted.

## Vision

I like to refer to having a vision for each of your goals as
forward and futuristic thinking. Vision is having a mental
picture of what you are trying to achieve. Vision tells you where
you are going, and when you have a vision of where you are
going in life, school, or work, your vision provides you with
personal security and direction. Every successful individual I've
ever met or read about has had a vision to help him or her to
achieve greatness in life, school, & work. Your vision must be
extremely clear because if you have a fuzzy vision, I guarantee
you that your path to success will be filled with distraction,
disorder, and chaos.

## Goals

A goal is a specific target where effort and energy are aimed
and directed. In a group or team environment, the definition
remains the same with one exception—the group or team as a
whole must agree upon the goal. The group must collectively
focus their efforts and energies on the agreed upon target,
which is the group's common bond. The wonderful thing
about goals is that they provide guidance and directions for

people. Goals provide outlines that tell you what you should be doing daily enroute to fulfilling your dreams and aspirations. Goals will also dictate how and where you spend your time. In the process of writing this book, I definitely knew from week to week where I would be spending my time. Yes, I had playtime, but I also had to work a lot to accomplish this goal.

Specific goals tell you what *you* need to be doing every step of the way in the goal achieving process. Goals with a purpose allow you to save valuable time and energy because you know and understand the underlying motivation for your actions. Goals with a purpose significantly reduce your chances of losing focus, becoming distracted, and habitually procrastinating.

Now that you have a better understanding of goals with purpose and vision, you can explore where you are personally in regards to achieving your goals in life, school, & work. Based on quantifiable research, personal interviews of successful and unsuccessful people, observations, and personal experiences, I will share with you ten reasons why people do not set goals and, therefore, become unsuccessful in life, school, & work. I refer to these ten reasons throughout the book as **barriers to success**. In the last section of this book, I'll offer eight steps to making success happen in life, school, & work. The rest is up to you, so *Get Up Off Your Butt & Do It NOW!*

# Part 2:
## The Three Keys to Motivation

# 1. Dream, Imagine, and Think

All businesses, creations, and inventions first start in the mind. It is in our dreams, imagination, and thoughts that we give birth to whatever it is we want out of life, school, & work. There is no need to be motivated if we have nothing to pursue or be motivated towards; we must have a goal in mind in order to achieve success. The first key to motivation is actually developing a mental awareness (picture) of what we want, and that starts with being aware of the creations of the mind. So what is it that you want out of life, school, & work? What do you want to be when you grow up? How do you want to make your living? Yes, you have an entrepreneurial spirit, and you want to chart your own course in life by being your own boss and starting a very successful business, but the question remains, what kind of business do you want to start?

If we dream it, imagine it, and think it, then it can be done and accomplished. The great Albert Einstein once said, "Imagination is more important than knowledge." Mr. Einstein knew that with every idea generated from our imaginations, human kind would only produce a larger pool of knowledge. Whenever you see a unique business, creation, or invention, remember it started in the mind first. The goal is to spend time dreaming, imagining, and thinking about what you really want. The ideas you have conceived and given birth to during the thinking process are only successful when you put action behind each one of your ideas. All ideas must be accompanied with actions and energy to support them—if not, they remain as dreams only. Srully Blotnick, Ph.D., an investment counselor, illustrated this by remarking, "The average person stumbles upon at least four ideas a year, any of which, if it were acted upon, might render vast wealth."

I was first introduced to this concept in 2000 while listening to Dr. Dennis P. Kimbro's audiotape "What Makes the

Great Great." To this day, I still don't understand how Dr. Blotnick and Dr. Kimbro came up with the concept that we get at least four ideas a year, but here's what I do believe and know: "Nothing happens unless first there's a dream," according to Carl Sandburg, twentieth-century American author.

Your dreams, thoughts, and images will carry and guide you throughout life, school, & work. One of my favorite proverbs is Proverbs 29:18 (KJV): "Where there is no vision, the people perish." I believe that people die emotionally, mentally, physically, and spiritually when they have nothing to live for in life. I remember a few years ago, I went home to Chicago to visit my family, and I was spending time with one of my favorite uncles. When I was growing up, he became my father figure when my biological father wasn't around. He was the father who took me swimming, to the museums, and on other excursions, so I developed a special place for him in my heart. This uncle was full of energy, and he lived life to the fullest when I was younger, but as I got older, I realized his zest and spunk for life were gone. I asked him what happened to his zest. As we sat in my mother's front room, he squeamishly put his head down and said, "I gave up, and I've been depressed for years."

I responded by saying, "You are only forty-four years old. You still have life inside of you." I quickly added, "You still have about thirty to forty years left inside of you…. Let's go for a drive," and we drove down Roosevelt Road in Chicago, endlessly discussing his situation and working on a game plan to get him out of his rut.

I asked him if he had ever heard of the movie title *Dead Man Walking*. He responded by saying no, but he said the movie title was a reflection of his life. I told him I agreed with him. I told him he was physically alive, but he was just waiting to be buried. I said, "You are physically alive, but you are mentally, emotionally, and spiritually dead." This is why it is so important to have a vision. Without vision, we are not really living.

Your personal vision, dreams, and thoughts will breathe life into you and will prolong your life on earth because they provide purpose, energy, and passion. Having a vision, dreaming, and thinking of the future is what kept Dr. Viktor E. Frankl alive in the Auschwitz concentration camp in Germany. He states in his landmark bestseller *Man's Search for Meaning*, "When we saw a comrade smoking his own cigarettes, we knew he had given up faith in his strength to carry on, and, once lost, the will to live seldom returned." Cigarettes were a hot commodity in the concentration camps; they could be exchanged for twelve servings of soups, which, of course, prevented starvation. Smoking one's cigarettes instead of trading them for food meant the person had lost his/her will to survive. Dr. Frankl said there was one thing (his personal vision for his life) that kept him alive even when he saw friends and family members around him wither away, die, or be taken off to the gas chambers. He says, "Every man was controlled by one thought only: to keep himself alive for the family at home, and to save his friends." That was his vision. We should also keep our vision alive not only for ourselves but also for those we love and care about around us. I would like to leave you with one of my favorite poems by Langston Hughes:

*Hold fast to dreams,*

*For if dreams die,*

*Life is a broken-winged bird,*

*That cannot fly.*

*Hold fast to dreams,*

*For when dreams go,*

*Life is a barren field,*

*Frozen with snow.*

Whenever I think of this poem, I think of how important it is to get a tight and firm grip on our dreams and goals because they have the power to carry us into the future. Langston

Hughes was known for addressing discrimination and racial tension between the 1920s to the 1960s and for writing colorful portrayals of black life in America during the Harlem Renaissance (an African-American cultural movement between the 1920s and 1930s, centered in Harlem, New York, that celebrated the black voice, the black tradition, and the black way of life). Langston Hughes understood what the power of a dream could do for people, but I believe he also observed many people give up on their dreams. Perhaps they gave on their dreams and aspirations because they were sick and tired of fighting against discrimination, racial inequalities, and unfair business, education, employment, and housing practices. However, Langston held fast to his dream and took the road less traveled and became a catalyst for human rights and social equality issues.

## 2. Make a Decision

After you have dreamed, imagined, and thought about what is it you really want out of life, school, & work, the second key to motivation is to make a final decision and begin to act on your decision. Brian Tracy in his videotape program *10 Keys to A More Powerful Personality* says, "80 percent of Americans are indecisive." One week I asked 150 of my communication students if they agreed with Mr. Tracy's statement, and about 95 percent of the students agreed with him. I went further into the discussion with them by asking, "Why do you think so many people are indecisive in life, school, & work?"

Here were the top three responses, and I've paraphrased them:

1. People are afraid of being wrong and making mistakes.

2. People fear what others might say or think about their decisions.

3. People haven't slowed down enough to think about what they really want out of life, school, & work. They are just going through the daily motions of living and surviving.

I believe the best way to start making decisions is simply to start making decisions. I say decide what you want and begin to go after your goal. Yet, some people get stuck or become indecisive when they have multiple dreams and ideas they want to pursue.

The best way to deal with this indecision is to make a list of the pros and cons to each idea, then ask yourself what are the benefits and liabilities of each idea or particular goal. There are three factors you must keep in mind after you have weighed your options for your ideas, and they are passion, time, and resources. What idea or goal do you feel passionate about pursuing? You cannot be wishy-washy when making this decision.

I encountered my own need for passion regarding my ideas while in graduate school. I had three topics in mind when I was considering what my thesis research paper or project would be. I was enrolled in a graduate seminar class, and the chair of the speech communications department encouraged all students to pick a topic we felt very passionate about. His exact words were, "Pick a topic that you would love to make love to all night and all day and that you wouldn't mind waking up to in the morning." When I heard those words, I knew exactly where I was going to spend my time researching and writing. So I ask you, which of your ideas or goals do you want to make love to, wake up to, and go to bed with? Follow your passion. Which idea or goal will you commit and dedicate yourself to while still balancing and honoring the other activities going on in your life? You won't be able to pursue every goal; you must be realistic about what you can handle and deliver on.

I already had a busy schedule, but I knew I could write this book on the weekends and during the wee hours of the mornings, and I guess it helps that I am a morning person. You must make time if you are truly committed to your goals and ideas. Finally, ask yourself if you have the resources or if you can get the resources to implement one of your ideas or goals within a reasonable amount of time. During the goal-achieving process, it is rather critical to get a few small successes, wins, and victories under your belt because they increase self-esteem, commitment, and participation. Eventually, the average person gives up rather easily if he or she keeps running into roadblocks while going after his or her goals. So don't set yourself up for failure. Pick a task, goal, or idea you can actually implement.

Zig Ziglar says it best about making a decision, "You can't hit a target you cannot see, and you cannot see a target you do not have." Ask yourself, based on the decision you've made, "At what target am I aiming my efforts and energies?" The most important aspect of goal achieving is that you must have a goal in place. After you have made your decision, ask yourself, "Am I willing to do whatever it takes to fulfill my dream?" Ultimately your choices, not your circumstances, or situations, will determine your level of success in life, school, & work.

## 3. Never Allow for an Interception or Interference to Take Place

It was fall semester of 1997 when I received my first full-time teaching assignment at a two-year technical college in Minnesota in the speech department. One of my many tasks on the first day of each semester was to make an immediate bond and connection with my students, so I created an icebreaker that allowed me to get to know the students better. There were ten fill-in-the-blank statements I asked each student to answer. They could skip any questions they didn't feel comfortable answering, but they had to answer a minimum of three questions. My two favorite questions and the two most popular among the students were:

1. If you had $10,000 tax-free, what would you do with the money?

2. If you could do it all over again, what would you do differently?

Now I'm not Sigmund Freud or a renowned psychoanalyst, but I believed the first question gave me a little insight into the students' personal values. The second statement, which I was most interested in, gave me more insight about their past regrets in life and their desires to rectify past mistakes or wrongs.

Here's what I found in teaching twenty to thirty courses within those three years: Approximately 85 to 90 percent of those students stated, "IF I could do it all over again, I would have taken my education more serious early on, and I would have listened more attentively to my parents' advice when they were trying to steer me in the right direction when I was younger." I taught all evening and late afternoon courses during this time, and the median age in the classroom was thirty-three. The majority of these students fit one or more of these variables: full-time working adults, married, one or more kids, and working towards a degree to move up the organizational ladder with their current employer. When students would discuss in detail what they meant, the common denominator I extracted from their responses was that they had allowed interceptions and interferences to prevent their goals from being achieved early on in life and school.

An interception or interference is any barrier, obstacle, or stumbling block YOU allow to stop you or cut you off from reaching your desired destination. Many people allow themselves—as you will discover later in the book—other people, and certain circumstances and events to intercept and interfere with their dreams, goals, and aspirations. So the third key to motivation is to NEVER allow for an interception or interference to take place while on the journey to accomplishing your goals in life, school, & work. I often share with friends, students, and workshop participants that our intimate partners, along with family members and friends, have been responsible for a lot of goal interference in life, school, & work. Remember, we personally allow this goal interference to happen. When we get caught up in our emotions for certain individuals that we care a great deal about, it is easy to forget about our dreams, goals, and aspirations. Our dreams and goals end up on the back burner because we postpone them. Sometimes we lose sight because love is blind—sometimes we don't want to see or believe that the people we love the most may be the greatest hindrance to our success in life.

I have heard countless stories from people in bad marriages and horrible relationships who say, "I wish I wouldn't have wasted my time with that person because they only tore me down." So many people leave relationships with regrets because the relationship drained them so much mentally, emotionally, and physically that they never even thought about themselves or their goals. They spent so much time trying to make the relationship work that they didn't have time to do anything else. They were so busy they neglected to work on their personal dreams and goals.

Some people allow certain life events to stop them and cut them off from accomplishing their goals. There will be times when you will have to adjust, re-adjust, adjust, and re-adjust again, but you must never allow an interception or interference to stop you completely. People, circumstances, and events may stop you temporarily, but you are the only person who can stop you permanently. In order for you to keep on keeping on while going through the challenges in your life, you must develop perseverance and a stick-to-it-ness mentality. I love when Sean "P-Ditty" Combs encourages fans and listeners at the end of certain records, NOT to STOP chasing and going after each and every one of their goals in life, school, & work. That's the stick-to-it-ness mentality that is needed when times get tough, and, believe me, they will get tough, but you must keep going towards your goals despite all levels of adversity.

There's a verse in the Bible that I really like, and it supports the stick-to-it-ness mentality. It simply states in Romans 14:5 (KJV), "Let every man be fully persuaded in his own mind." I like to say, "Let every man and every woman be fully persuaded about what they really want out of life, school, & work." Avoid being double-minded; there's a scripture in James 1:8 (KJV) that also says that "a doubled-minded man is unstable in all of his ways." Dream, imagine, and think about what you really want. You need to keep the three keys of motivation in mind in order to stay motivated. Make a final decision to pursue that particular dream, goal, or idea. Sometimes in the process of reaching for our goals, life challenges can get in the way. These life challenges are explained in this book as the Ten Barriers to Success. I believe a problem is 50 percent solved once you have identified the root cause of the problem. Once you have identified which barriers are sabotaging your success in life, school, or work; you can learn strategies to overcome these barriers. These Ten barriers are the most common interceptions or interferences you may encounter. Exploring and understanding which of these Ten barriers you struggle with will help you remember that while you are on the road to success, you should never allow for an interception or interference to keep you from achieving your goals and dreams.

# Part 3:
## Ten Barriers that Prevent Success from Happening

# Barrier 1:
# People Do Not See and Understand the Importance of Goal Setting

The first reason people do not set goals is that they do not see and understand the importance of goal setting. Over 95 percent of our population have not embraced the importance goals have to enable and empower them to truly succeed in life, school, & work. People have existed and lived for decades, even centuries, without ever consciously setting concrete goals for themselves. Yes, it is possible to have minimal successes in life, school, & work without ever setting a single goal. However, you can accomplish more and gain more with goals than without goals because goals give you a sense of meaning, purpose, and direction.

## Keys to effectiveness

In studying the lives of successful and unsuccessful people, I have observed an important element: Successful people accomplish, achieve, and succeed more often because they follow a well-planned, well-organized, and well-structured system that can be duplicated. Unsuccessful people sometimes get what they want by pure luck or mere chance. Unsuccessful people do not follow a game plan, blueprint, or structured system. The major distinction here is that one group creates opportunities for themselves while the other group waits for opportunities instead of creating opportunities for themselves.

### Being Proactive

The process of taking initiative and personal action to make positive events happen and take place in your life is called proactivity. In contrast, reactivity is the process of waiting for something or someone else to make positive events or outcomes to happen for you in your life. Events happen in your life. Now ask yourself, am I a proactive or reactive person? Your answer will determine the height of your success in life, school, & work.

To get the most out of life, you must first become effective constantly. Effectiveness is accomplishing and achieving your desired results. Effectiveness is the key; effectiveness is the ability to get what you want over and over again by following a well-planned and structured system, not by relying on pure luck or mere chance. I call this process the **Cycle of Duplication**—that is, getting what you want over and over again by following a well-planned and well-structured system.

The **Cycle of Duplication** consists of two steps:

**Step 1** You must develop a personal formula (which is your step-by-step plan of action) to follow consistently for each goal you plan to accomplish.

**Step 2** Every goal has three phases: the beginning, the middle, and the end. You must understand and master each phase if the cycle of duplication is to be effective and successful.

**An example of the Cycle of Duplication:** First, one of the main principles of success is to fully understand what created or made your success in the first place. Haphazard success cannot be duplicated because there is no pattern to the process to follow, but success with a game plan can consistently be duplicated.

For instance, let's say Margaret opens a 24-hour laundromat because she believes this kind of business venture will generate a monthly cash flow to contribute to her retirement fund. She invests 75 percent of her savings into the business, and after seven and one-half months of being in business, she must file for bankruptcy because Margaret doesn't have enough operating capital. For the Cycle of Duplication to work, Margaret must spend some time researching and figuring out what caused her business to fail.

As she backtracks over the months, here's what she discovers as factors that contributed to her business failing: Her laundromat was in a commercial location rather than a residential area of the city, she over priced her competition for washing and drying services, she failed to aggressively market and promote her new business (she thought opening the doors with three press releases would be enough for marketing and promotions), she didn't have any give-aways to attract customers or a grand opening, and she spent too much money on payroll for a 24-hour laundry operation (she didn't have enough customers to justify staying open 24 hours). A year later, Margaret reopens the business under another name and avoids all the costly mistakes that caused her to fail a year earlier. Not only does the new laundromat become a success, but she also opens three others within a three-year period. How does she do it? She follows the Cycle of Duplication. She uses the same format and formula for the latter three laundromats, and she vows to follow the same process for each and every laundromat she plans to open up in the future.

**Remember** the key to goal setting and goal achieving is learning and knowing how to get what you want over and over again according to a systematic game plan. Without blueprints to follow, most goals never happen or even begin construction.

# Barrier 2
# People Have Not Been Taught How to Set Goals

The second reason people do not set goals is that they have never been taught how to set goals. Here is the simplicity of Barrier 2: No one can set a goal if they have never been formally introduced to or taught the concepts of goal setting and goal achieving. However, in order to teach a person anything, the teacher must first be skilled at the task or subject. I define *skill* as knowing how to perform a task successfully based on training, practice, and repeated experience. So for someone to teach another person the skill of goal setting, first he or she must have learned the skill of goal setting from someone who has had many successful experiences in setting and achieving personal and professional goals. Because people can only teach what they know, people can only give away what they possess. Simply put, I can't lend you $25.00 if I ain't got it! You or I cannot teach goal setting and goal achievement if we don't possess the skill set of goal setting and goal achievement.

## Personal experience

While growing up, I was never taught the process of goal setting. As a matter of fact, I did not learn to set goals until my early twenties. See, my mother never taught any of her four children to set goals. Remember you can only teach what you have been taught. My grandmother did not teach my mother or her five brothers and sisters how to set goals because no one ever taught my grandmother the process of goal setting.

When I completed my first audiotape, I sent my grandmother an autographed copy. After attending church one Sunday, she listened to the audio book, called me, and stated, "I have something to talk to you about." My heart and emotions were immediately gripped with fear and anxiety; I began to backtrack mentally attempting to figure out what might have upset her because the tone in her voice sounded really troubling to me. She said, "Grandson, I'm sorry, and I want to apologize to you for not teaching your mother how to set goals." She said, "I didn't teach her because no one ever taught me how to set goals, so I didn't have the knowledge to teach your mother what I did not know how to do."

### The domino effect

As you can see, this domino effect can have a very dangerous impact on a family's future success. Just like destructive or negative family traditions, bad habits—like failing to set goals—can be passed down from one generation to another generation until someone finally breaks the cycle. I happened to break the cycle in my family, and now I can teach my family members, friends, students, children-to-come, and individuals such as you about the process of goal setting and goal achieving.

**Remember** if you change nothing, then nothing changes.

# Barrier 3
# People Simply Don't Know How to Pursue Goals

The third reason people do not set goals is simply because they do not know how to begin going after their goals once they've made a decision. This is where most confusion and perplexity takes place in the goal setting process. A significant number of people become frustrated and get stuck in the process of trying to figure out and decide what to do first, second, or third. I most often hear people say, "I wish I knew how to get started— I just don't know how to begin." The key to preventing this barrier from stealing your dreams and goals is to simply start. That's right, just start. I say start the process of doing something towards your goals and while in the process of motion you'll learn what to do next. William Shakespeare once said, "Great is the art of beginning."

## Lack of know-how is no excuse for goal achievers

Steven K. Scott, author of the book *A Millionaire's Notebook*, states, "Lack of know-how is without a doubt the single, greatest perceived obstacle to extraordinary achievement for the vast majority of American adults."

I agree with Mr. Scott 1,000 percent. I speak at conferences and work with thousands of people each year who watch and allow their dreams to fade away and their goals to die because they become disappointed and frustrated with not knowing how to start the process. They become so frustrated with the lack of not knowing how to pursue their goals that they give up and quit. They soon find themselves returning to their old ways and practices. Ignorance simply means lacking knowledge in a specific area. Rest assured, at some point in our human existence, we all—and I mean all—face our own lack of not knowing how to do something in a particular area. The goal is to eradicate and overcome ignorance with education.

## Two strategies for overcoming the lack of know-how

American humorist, twentieth-century writer, and social and political commentator, Will Rogers once said, "We are all ignorant, only on different subjects." So how do we overcome this problem of not knowing how to pursue goals? Are you ready for this super-complex-scientific answer? You overcome not knowing how to pursue goals by simply learning how to set goals. The goal is to research and seek out the best approaches, methods, and practices for accomplishing your goals. You learn how to do whatever you want to do in life by studying; listening to audio books; taking personal development courses; joining professional associations; attending conferences, seminars, and workshops; watching television specials such as biographies and documentaries; interviewing experts; and reading books, magazines, and newspaper articles. Finally, you learn by asking questions. As adults, we must relearn and understand that it is okay to ask questions if we lack sufficient knowledge in a particular area. When people lack sufficient knowledge in a particular area, everything appears difficult until they gain sufficient knowledge. Don Miguel Ruiz supports this perspective by stating in one of my favorite books, *The Four Agreements*, "If you don't understand, ask. Have the courage to ask questions until you are clear as you can be.... If you don't understand something it is better for you to ask and be clear, instead of making an assumption." Whenever knowledge is lacking, you better believe ignorance is waiting right around the corner to take its place. As rap icon, actor, and entertainer, Tupac Shakur, once said, "Even a genius asks questions."

## My thoughts

We can change the destructive and negative habits of making assumptions by adopting new constructive and positive habits of asking questions. I define a *habit* as an ingrained behavior that has been repeatedly practiced and learned over a period of time. We can change any habit we desire by following the four steps explained in part four, step two of the book, entitled "Needs Analysis."

I will close this section with a thought and a quote by actress Bo Derek, "The best investment is in you. If you think education is expensive, try ignorance."

# Barrier 4
## Setting Goals Requires Too Much Effort

The fourth reason people do not set goals is because goal achievement requires too much effort for some individuals. Too much effort is my "politically correct" phrase for saying people are too lazy to put in the necessary time and energy to get what they really want out of life, school, & work. There is one thing I want to be forthright and up-front about: Going after what you want in life will require you to take action. There are no shortcuts on the road to success. You must pay your dues and put in the required time and necessary energy for each one of your goals. Your time and energy requirements will vary from goal to goal because each goal is different. It takes a lot of determination, mental fortitude, and perseverance to accomplish your life goals, and you must pay the price for each of your goals. I encourage you to personally sit down and calculate the cost of each of your goals; then ask yourself, "Am I willing to pay the price?" In his book *The 17 Indisputable Laws of Teamwork*, Dr. John C. Maxwell says, "Individuals fail to reach their potential when they fail to pay the price." When it comes to fulfilling our hearts' desires and dreams, we must pay the price daily.

## Four Es of goal setting

Honestly speaking, some individuals are not willing to pay the price or to practice the **Four Es** of achieving their goals. The four Es are as follows:

1. The will to put in the required *effort*.

2. The *energy* needed to put in this effort.

3. The ability to *exert* yourself when opportunities knock at your door or when there are no knocks at all.

4. The ability to maintain a constant and consistent level of *enthusiasm*.

The four Es are essential to the mental and physical preparation you must possess on your journey to achieving your goals. But some individuals would whine, complain, and wait around for free rides in life rather than put forth the effort, energy, exertion, and enthusiasm needed to accomplish their goals in life, school, & work.

Working maximum hours to accomplish a goal and developing a strong work ethic are foreign concepts to the lazy. This is especially true for those who were spoiled as children and for those who were never taught to be accountable, responsible, and self-reliant. Individuals who possess these traits have a terrible work ethic for two reasons:

**Reason #1:** They have never had to work hard or perhaps work at all.

**Reason #2:** Their parents or guardians have made life too easy for them.

Investment billionaire Warren Buffet calls it "corporate suicide" when financially well-to-do parents spoil their children with riches and material things without ever teaching them the principle and value of hard work. Therefore, these individuals develop unhealthy, unproductive habits of dependency, laziness, neediness, and sometimes even disgusting attitudes of ungratefulness.

## A late night defining moment for me

This reminds me of a roommate I had in college. I had always regarded this particular roommate as extremely privileged. He was given a nice vehicle; his parents told him they did not want him to work because they wanted him to focus on his studies and grades. They even deposited a weekly allowance into a special checking account for him, and to top it off, he did not have to do his own laundry. I was envious of him at the time because I felt my life struggles were unfair compared to his life-style. I had to work a part-time job twenty to twenty-five hours a week and travel on the city bus in the blustery cold winters of Chicago. I had no financial support from my family, and I had to do my own laundry.

Late one night while studying for a biology exam, I had a defin-ing moment. It was about 1:00 a.m., and my roommate awakened from his sleep and said, "Jermaine, do you think I'm spoiled?"

I replied, "Yeah, just a little." I was minimizing how I really felt because I did not want to offend him.

His response was, "I know you look at me and wish you were in my shoes, but I really wish that I were in your shoes."

I said, "You're crazy, man, why would you want my life, and why would you want to be in my shoes?"

His reply was, "Because you know how to struggle, you know how to survive. I've watched you, Jermaine, and I wish I could do what you do. If my parents died today, I wouldn't know what to do." From that day on, I realized there were severe consequences of being spoiled and having parents or guardians who always bailed you out when you were faced with life chal-lenges. I believe my roommate desired to be independent but he learned to become dependent and his privileged way of life robbed him of this experience. I believe the Eastern philosophy says it best, "Give a man a fish and he'll eat for a day—teach a man to fish an he'll eat for a life time."

## Remember what you need to achieve your goals

$$\left.\begin{array}{l} \text{Effort} \\ \text{Energy} \\ \text{Exertion} \\ \text{Enthusiasm} \end{array}\right\} = \textit{Motivation \& Participation in Your Goals}$$

# Barrier 5
# People Have a Low Self-Concept

The fifth reason people fail to set goals is that they have a low self-concept.

## I *can't* do it

I once had a student named Cindy who took a twelve-week public speaking course with me. For the first four weeks of the course, Cindy tormented herself with her fears and insecurities about not being able pass the class. Her exact words were, "I can't do it. I cannot give a speech in front of you and those twenty-eight students. The last time I gave a speech was five years ago, and I threw up in front of the entire class, and I know—I *know* I'll do it again."

The funny thing about her belief and our conversation was that I totally agreed with Cindy. Initially, she was shocked and a little offended by my response. I told her she was absolutely correct in her estimation of not being able to pass the public speaking class if she maintained her low self-concept. I shared my beliefs and scholarly research with her regarding individuals with a low self-concept and the negative effect it can have on their performances in life, school, & work. I also shared two of my favorite quotes with Cindy. The first was a Biblical scripture taken from Proverbs 23:7 (KJV): "For as he [she] thinketh in his [her] heart, so is he [she]." The second quote was from the famous car manufacturer Henry Ford, "If you think you can, you can. And if you think you can't, you can't. Either way you're right."

## Self-concept

Self-concept is the way you see yourself. I like to refer to the self-concept as the Polaroid picture you carry of yourself inside your head. In his book *Self-Matters*, Dr. Phillip C. McGraw defines self-concept as, "The bundle of beliefs, facts, opinions, and perceptions about yourself that you travel through life with, every moment of every day." For example, if you truly believe you will be successful in whatever you choose to do, then you will not allow anything to stand in your way, no matter what happens, because you believe in yourself. Consequently, if you believe you will never achieve greatness in life, school, or work, then guess what? You won't.

There is a principle in general psychology that teaches us that people will always act and behave in a manner consistent with their dominant beliefs and thoughts. In other words, there is a direct correlation between what people most often think about and what they eventually act on. I found this to be true growing up in the slums and ghettos of Chicago's West Side. I have friends, former neighbors, and family members who will never rise above their negative circumstances as long as they continue to think and believe they are destined to be of a lower class and status in life. They will never rise above their low wages, low-income housing levels, and low social status if they persist in believing "This is the way the Man Upstairs wanted my life to be, and I'm just accepting the cards I was dealt in this game of life." I like to refer to this kind of thinking and processing as, the "Just to Get By Mentality" also known as the "Poverty Mentality."

## Changing our image of self

I have a belief I hold so deeply that I am willing to put my life on the line for it: People can hold you back or keep you down temporarily or momentarily, but *you* are the only person who can hold you back or keep you down permanently. If you want to change your actions or behaviors, you must first change the way you see yourself by changing the images and pictures you currently have of yourself in your mind. The more successes, wins, and victories you have in life, school, & work, the more your self-image and self-concept improves positively, just like the more failures and losses you have in life, school, & work, the more these kinds of events contribute to a negative self-image and self-concept. The more you experience successes, wins, and victories, the more the Polaroid picture inside of your head begins to change for the better. Find your passion, a hobby, or line of work you excel and thrive in, and I guarantee you that you will see a change in your self-image and self-concept.

## Success and the power of belief

I am very proud to say that Cindy, my public speaking student who did not believe she could do it, went on to pass the public speaking class she once feared and dreaded. She did more than pass the class—she earned a B+, and I know for certain she could not have achieved her goal without *believing* she could give a successful speech. She had to visualize herself giving five successful speeches in front of twenty-eight classmates and a professor who truly believed in her. Congratulations, Cindy, for making your dream come true by turning the negative perception you had of yourself into a positive one.

# Barrier 6
# Fear of Failure

The sixth reason people fail to set goals is that they have a fear of failure. I remember when I first realized that it was okay to be less than perfect. I was visiting a relative, and I witnessed a toddler in the beginning stages of walking. The toddler was trying to walk, and he consistently fell on the floor like toddlers often do. As the child kept falling, I heard my uncle's loud voice projecting from the kitchen area yelling, "Don't cry, don't cry; if you first don't succeed, try again."

Initially, I doubt the toddler was paying much attention to my uncle's words of encouragement. But the child seemed to understand my uncle's words, and after falling several times, the toddler eventually stood up and walked. He accomplished his goal! I wish more adults would embrace the determined and persistent attitude of that toddler. If so, more dreams and goals would be fulfilled in life, school, & work.

## Embrace failure as a step towards success

The fear of failure is the fear of making mistakes and the fear of taking risks. Fear of failure is created internally due to self-imposed emotional and psychological barriers. The fear of failure is created externally when our loved ones and professional colleagues put pressure on people to be unrealistically perfect. They may not create an environment for people to feel safe at failing, making mistakes, or dropping the ball at times. The fear of failure incapacitates, immobilizes, and prevents people from taking risks in life. When people willingly submit to the fear of failure and do not take chances or risks, they surrender their will to their fears and insecurities by playing it safe. They live life within the same bubble their entire lives without ever knowing how great they could possibly become. When people don't take risks, they never really know what they could become in life, school, or work.

The fear of failure is extremely dangerous; its grip is firm and tight. It compels and forces individuals to lead unhealthy lives by staying in destructive relationships, marriages, and careers. Simply stated, it prevents people from moving forward and taking positive action when they really need to. When we overcome the fear of failure, we unleash our authentic potential because we are emotionally and psychologically liberated to be creative, innovative, and explorative. This liberation creates endless possibilities in life, school, & work.

### Failure in life is inevitable

I believe part of the human experience while on planet Earth is to experience failure and resistance. We all miss the mark at times; we all encounter defeats and make foolish mistakes, both consciously and unconsciously. It is extremely abnormal not to fail. As psychologist Dr. Joyce Brothers states, "The person interested in success has to learn to view failure as a healthy, inevitable part of the process of getting to the top." Statistically speaking, we are more likely to fail than to succeed as we set out to accomplish our dreams and goals in life.

Once again, failure happens to everyone; failure is an event, not a person or personal attribute. Failures are occurrences, moments, occasions, episodes, and incidents we all experience on our journey in life. Over two hundred years ago, Alexander Pope wrote an essay entitled "Criticism," and an often quoted phrase comes from that essay that reinforces the belief that failure is part of the human experience, "To err is human, to forgive divine."

My personal experience with "failure" came as a student. My very first semester of college, I nearly failed. I was enrolled in four classes, and I received three Cs in three of my classes and an F in my fourth which was Biology. I had a GPA of 1.5, a D+ average, which is unacceptable according to the academic standards of Elmhurst College. On paper, I was a loser and a failure, but in reality, I wasn't. Three years later, I graduated a semester early and enrolled in graduate school. I had experienced a moment, an occasion, an episode, or an incident in my life where I experienced the event of failure. But, in the long run, I, Jermaine M. Davis, the *person*, was not a failure.

### Failure is an event

I want to plant a seed with hopes that it will grow inside your subconscious and conscious mind until it is fully developed. Failure is an event that happens to us all, and it is not a personal character flaw that some possess and others do not. An entrepreneur who really understands the concept of failure as an event and not a person is Jim McCann, the entrepreneur who created and started the very successful company, 1-800 Flowers. Mr. McCann includes a chapter in his book *Stop and Smell the Roses* entitled "The Art of Making Mistakes." Imagine that! He was a social worker in New York for over twenty years and then decided to become a CEO and entrepreneur. In his book, he states, "Show me a business person who says he or she doesn't make mistakes, and I'll show you a liar." Everybody makes mistakes. If you do not make mistakes, then you are not taking the necessary risks that will lead you toward higher goals.

### Entrepreneurs take risks

Becoming an entrepreneur is all about taking risks. Taking a risk means that sometimes you make a mistake, but making mistakes does not imply that you are a failure. According to Tulane University business professor Lisa Amos, "The average for entrepreneurs is 3.8 failures before they finally make it in business." These individuals are not discouraged by adversity because they have learned from all of their failures and adversities. Truthfully speaking, there are valid reasons why some individuals have a fear of failure, but these fears are their stumbling blocks—the barriers that prevent them from accomplishing their goals in life, school, & work.

## Why we fear failure

One of the main reasons people have a fear of failure is that, as children, we were not taught that it was okay to fail and make mistakes on the road to success and greatness. Perhaps we were not fortunate enough to grow up in a household where we were encouraged to learn from our failures and mistakes. Most people were never told that most successful people actually failed their way to success. Some individuals grew up in environments where their parents reacted neutrally to success but punished a child for failure. This form of parenting explains why some individuals fear failing and avoid taking risks in life. Some people were regularly reprimanded and sometimes severely punished for mishaps, missteps, and shortcomings. For example, we may have been reprimanded when we did not tie our shoes correctly, if we spilled pop or juice on the kitchen floor, or for receiving only a C in a class. We may have worked really hard, but our parents did not recognize our effort and hard work because they were blinded by their personal agenda of perfectionism and became disappointed when their kids did not receive an A or a B. When we made the typical blunders that all youths make, we felt like failures and losers. The fear of failure usually begins when our individual efforts do not meet or match the expectations of significant people in our lives.

## The Avoidance Motive

At the heart and core of the fear of failure is "The Avoidance Motive." The fear of failure can become so strong that individuals will go to great lengths to avoid the criticisms and reprimands of the people who are important and close to them, such as parents, siblings, teachers, close friends, and employers. They will not take risks for fear of letting others down and for fear of not being successful in their personal and professional endeavors.

When we are punished for honest, innocent, and sincere mistakes, we are more likely to withdraw from risk taking situations entirely. We tend to avoid any situation where we may be unsuccessful. Why is this? Because we do not want to feel the ugly, nasty, dirty, uncomfortable, and negative feelings and emotions associated with being a failure. According to psychologist Dr. David McClelland, those who have a high fear of failure are extremely afraid for two reasons:

1. They fear verbal criticism, and

2. They fear punishment for the failure itself.

Their negative internal dialogue begins to say, "I can't quit my job—what would my parents or friends think? I can't start that business—what would people say if the business fails or goes under?" Due to destructive feedback and negative verbal reprimands they've experienced in the past, some people avoid any potential mistakes in order to avoid failing or receiving negative feedback. For this very reason, some people have never set or pursued any goals for themselves in life, school, & work.

# Barrier 7
## Fear of Rejection

The seventh reason people fail to set goals is their fear of rejection.

Fear of rejection is the irrational belief that others will not accept you for who you are, what you believe, and how you act. It is a state of mind that prevents people from doing what they want to do and saying what they want to say—it prevents people from really being themselves. The fear of rejection is caused by the number one emotional need in life: the need for acceptance.

**The need for acceptance** has caused millions of people to sacrifice their own happiness and disregard their own principles, morals, needs, and values in order to make others happy. It is virtually impossible to please everyone, and trying to do so is an illusion. It can never happen; you can never achieve it. This is one of the most unachievable and unrealistic goals to ever consider.

## My mom's insight

As a youth, my mother, Carolyn Charmaine Davis, was the queen of using repetition to guarantee that her pearls of wisdom would stick inside my stubborn head. She would say, "J.D., baby, you can't please everyone. You have to learn to please yourself first. There will always be critics." She would also say, "When you are on the top, people talk about you. When you are in the middle, trying to determine what to do next, people talk about you. When you are on the bottom, people really talk about you and point fingers."

When I was growing up, I did not understand the value of my mom's words. However, I later realized that her message was filled with knowledge, wisdom, and lots of life experience. My interpretation of my mom's words: If I lived my life attempting to please others, I would not be successful in the game of life because trying to please everyone is an illusion that no one can attain.

## The formula for failure: Trying to please everyone

Remember, whether you are on top, in the middle, or at the bottom, there will always be people ready to scrutinize, criticize, and pass judgment. So what should you do? I suggest you live your life according to your deepest beliefs, values, and principles. Please remember to serve your best interests because you are Numero Uno, my friend. When you live to please others because you do not want to offend them or because you want to be liked and accepted by them, you primarily forsake yourself. When you forsake and neglect your own needs, you have just compromised your personal integrity as a person.

**Ask yourself:** Can you, or would you, respect someone who compromises important principles and denies their own happiness in order to win the acceptance and approval of others?

When asked about his personal formula for success on the *Larry King Live Show,* Mr. Bill Cosby—philanthropist, comedian, actor, one of America's favorite fathers, and the Jell-O Gelatin Man—replied, "I do not know the formula for success. But I do know the formula for failure, and that is trying to please everyone."

Millions of people live and operate their lives habitually wondering what others would say or think about the decisions they make for their OWN lives. They worry about what others think of them constantly. They are more concerned with what others think about their goals than about how they personally feel about their own dreams, goals, and aspirations. Their decisions are made, or not made, based on the beliefs and opinions of others. They try to please everyone—or, at least, to please the significant people in their lives—which is absolutely impossible. People will drive you crazy. You will lose your mind if you live your life like this, trying to please others and living your life to meet *their* expectations. By far, trying to please everyone is one of the most unreasonable and unrealistic goals a person could ever attempt to achieve. This is the recipe and formula for failure.

## Test yourself

I have a series of important questions for you to consider very closely:

- Do you know where the cure for cancer is?
- Do you know where the cure for AIDS is?
- Do you know where the cure for Alzheimer's Disease or Spinal Bifida is?
- Do you know where the cure for the common cold is?
- Do you know where to find the next multi-platinum-recording artist?
- Do you know where the next Academy and Grammy Award winners are?
- Do you know where the best inventors and the best inventions are located?

What if I told you that I knew where the answers were to all the above questions? Would you believe me? Probably not. Believe it or not, I really *do* know where the answers are located and exist, but I did not discover the answer on my own. One of my favorite motivational speakers, Les Brown, shared the answer with me in 1994 while I was in graduate school, sitting in my dorm room, watching his weekly PBS special.

Les Brown stated that the answers to all of these questions are "the grave." At first, I was a little perplexed by his answer. Then he began to elaborate and expound on how millions of people take their plans, desires, inventions, books, movies, songs, plays, discoveries, cures/remedies, solutions, and dreams to the grave with them because they possess a fear of rejection.

## What happens to a dream deferred?

Dr. Myles Munroe, author of *Understanding Your Potential*, takes Les Brown's statement a step further. Dr. Munroe states,

"The wealthiest spots on the planet are not the oil fields of Kuwait, Iraq, or Saudi Arabia. Neither is it the gold and diamond mines of South Africa, the uranium mines of the Soviet Union, or the silver mines of Africa. Though it may surprise you, the richest deposits on our planet lie just a few blocks from your house; they rest in your local cemetery or graveyard. Buried beneath the soil, within the walls of those sacred grounds, are dreams that never came to pass, songs that were never sung, books that were never written, paintings that never filled a canvas, ideas that were never shared, visions that never became reality, inventions that were never designed, plans that never went beyond the drawing board of the mind, and purposes that were never filled. Our graveyards are filled with potentials that remain potentials. What a tragedy."

### Two factors that cause the fear of rejection

What causes the fear of rejection to be so prevalent in the lives of millions of people? According to several psychologists in the book *Human Motivation*, two dominant factors contribute to fear of rejection:

1. The need for **affiliation**.
2. The need for **approval**.

Individuals with a high need for affiliation, and with a high need for approval, act and behave in ways that will create social acceptance and social approval for themselves from others. They will avoid any form of conflict or competition. These individuals experience a high level of rejection anxiety; they hate the thought of being rejected by anyone. They fear any form of feedback, even constructive feedback (which is the good stuff). Their prayers, hopes, and wishes are to avoid conflict and disagreements at any and all costs. They are constantly preoccupied with the thoughts and reactions of others in their personal and professional relationships. The people with a high need for affiliation and approval are so consumed and concerned with being liked by others that they lose focus on and sight of their own dreams, goals, and happiness.

***Real life examples***, I know two women who are extremely beautiful, both internally and externally. They desire to be models, but they will never pursue modeling careers because they have a huge fear of rejection. They are so concerned and worried about what others will think and say that they have put their potential modeling careers on the back burner as they read magazines and see new commercials everyday of models that are very comparable to them. I also have friends who are single, desiring to be in rich and meaningful relationships, but they are afraid to ask people out on dates because they fear they will be rejected.

These are only a few examples of people who do not set goals or achieve their dreams in life because of their debilitating and irrational fear of rejection.

# Barrier 8
# Fear of Success

The eighth reason people do not set goals is they have a fear of success. At the first thought of the phrase "fear of success" it would appear this concept is an oxymoron. I often think, "Who in their right frame of mind would oppose or reject any form of legitimate success?" The psychology behind the fear of success explains how this barrier sabotages, interferes with, and disrupts dreams, goals, and aspirations. So what is fear of success? It is disregarding, minimizing, and/or rejecting accomplishments and achievements due to the fear of social rejection.

## Success brings attention

In other words, it is not the success that people fear; it is the attention that success brings—such as acknowledgment, praise, prosperity, and recognition—that creates the fear. Those who have a fear of success do achieve greatness, but many times, they do not allow themselves to appreciate and celebrate their achievements. They afflict themselves with feelings of guilt, so they create situations for themselves that are simultaneously self-defeating and self-sabotaging.

*For example*, in the movie *Finding Forrester,* Academy Award winner Sean Connery plays a Pulitzer Prize writer and winner (William Forrester) who goes into seclusion after he has allowed his personal tragedies in life to make him bitter and angry at the world. Mr. Connery begins to mentor a young African-American kid named Jamal Wallace. In the movie, Jamal is raised in the inner city of New York where sports and street credibility are praised more than academic achievements.

However, Jamal is gifted with the pen and pad and exemplifies exceptional writing abilities. When his parents divorced early in his life, he developed his art and learned to write creatively to channel his thoughts and feelings of resentment on paper. However, Jamal exhibits a fear of success in high school because his peers begin to tease him about being really smart and being a teacher's pet. So Jamal goes from being an A student to an average C student. Remember, with the fear of success, it is not the success that people fear but the attention success brings.

## Psychologists say

Studies on the fear of success have shown that it really impacts and stifles women and people of color in the workplace. Research has shown that in achievement situations, women in the workplace did not always perform to their maximum potential when competing against men. Psychologist Dr. Horner best explains the reasons behind this in her documented study "A Psychological Barrier to Achievement in Women: The Motive to Avoid Success." She states, "Many psychologists believed women had much more anxiety over appearing aggressive and competitive than men did." In similar gender studies on the impact of the fear of success in secondary schools, psychologist Dr. Shinn shared similar views by stating, "Fear of success was inhibiting the performance of the girls now that they were in a situation where they were competing with boys, whereas before, when they were competing with girls, high levels of fear of success had not prohibited their performance. A similar shift did not occur for the boys."

As both psychologists pointed out, the fear of success is an emotional and psychological barrier that sabotages, interferes with, and interrupts achievements. We can see this when an individual begins to pursue his or her goals and something abruptly stops their drive and momentum. As Austrian psychoanalyst Sigmund Freud once said, "Those who fear success have an unconscious need to fail; not just a desire, but a need."

## So what are the thoughts of those with a fear of success?

- What if I cannot handle the new job or the extra responsibilities?

- Shouldn't I just play it safe and keep the job I have? I already make good money.

- I thought I was ready; I just need a few more months, and I'll be ready then.

- Aren't people going to treat me differently now that I got the new management position?

- Aren't people going to watch me and pay more attention to me now?

- Won't people want me to perform at this level all the time?

- Will people dislike me or become jealous of me when I become successful?

- There are lots of brighter, smarter, and more talented people than me.

## Fear of success—not me

During my first semester as a graduate student, I took a course on the psychology of human motivation. One of my many semester assignments was to write a research paper analyzing and describing my personal view of any fears that had hindered me in the past, that I presently confronted, or that I perceived to be challenges for me in the future.

The core question was what are the fears that hinder and block your successes in life? We were instructed to include all fears that were applicable within the guidelines of the assignment. My only real fear, my only giant, my only barrier, was the fear of failure. Or so I thought. I turned in my lengthy, academic and analytical research paper and received a B-. The professor, Dr. Carroll, remarked that I had only written on the fear of *failure*, but he was quite sure that I had at least one more fear, which he thought was the fear of success.

Immediately after class, I asked Dr. Carroll to explain his comments and the reasoning behind the grade. In his soft-spoken, mild-mannered way, he encouraged me to reread the section in our textbook on the fear of success. But no, I did not want to reread that section. I desired two results: an A and a verbal explanation detailing why I did not receive an A. I was 21, young, stubborn, and grossly opinionated. At the time, I did not understand what he was trying to show me, and I really did not care. I only wanted my grade changed, and I fiercely argued with him, insisting that I did not have a fear of success. Here I was in graduate school after almost dropping out my first semester of undergraduate school. I had successfully avoided the three Ps—parole, prison, and probation—discussed by Dr. Dennis P. Kimbro in his book *What Makes the Great, Great.* Growing up in inner city Chicago, I felt I had beaten the odds for young black males between the ages of 18 and 25, so I thought Dr. Carroll was out of his mind. I just knew I was on the road to success. I had graduated from high school in three years by the age of 17, completed my BA in three-and-one-half years by the age of 20, and I was on to completing my first Masters in one-and-one-half years by the age of 22. Dr. Carroll stood his ground, and he encouraged me to reread the chapter—but I refused to at the time.

Because I was fascinated with the topics of achievement, the psycholgy of winning, success, and the psychology of motivation, I continued to read, research, and attend seminars on the subject. One day I noticed something very peculiar: The phrase "fear of success" kept resurfacing in my life. The truth and wisdom behind Dr. Carroll's words became very clear and apparent to me when I received two career offers: to teach full-time at a technical college and to teach part-time at the University of Minnesota. Here it was, the opportunity I had longed for throughout my college career. This was finally it; this was what I had waited for;

prayed to the Creator about; and discussed passionately with my mentors, close friends, and family members. This was what I cried about when I was alone at home or driving in my car, thinking about my future goals and career aspirations. It was here. I had received the opportunity to become a college instructor of speech communication. Now I could quit all my meaningless jobs and focus on my professional teaching career in higher education. Yet, a shadow of doubt and fear hung over this new opportunity.

## Success will increase others' expectations of us

As I contemplated my new opportunity, I experienced fear—fear of success! Why did I have a fear of success? One reason was because of my age—I was 25 years young at the time, and nearly 90 percent of my students were older than me. So initially, my negative self-talk was telling me that I was too young to teach—that I was too inexperienced, incompetent, and inadequate. Since 90 percent of my students would also be white Americans, the question of race also frightened and concerned me. I began to second guess my talents, abilities, gifts, and skills with my negative self talk. I nearly drove myself crazy bombarding myself with this vision of a young black male teaching middle and older age white students in Minnesota.

I also had other negative thoughts roaming in my head:

- What if my students know more about the subject than I do?

- What if I really cannot break down and explain the theories and concepts in the class textbook?

- What if I am not prepared?

- What if I cannot answer the students' questions?

- What if I am not as smart and talented as I think I am?

- What if they disagree with my grading policy just as I once disagreed with Dr. Carroll's?

- What if my students respond negatively to my teaching style?

- What if I lose my thoughts right in the middle of my lectures?

- What if I am boring?

What if, what if, what if? These "what ifs" caused me many sleepless nights.

I believe we have a fear of success because we believe we will not be capable or competent enough to handle the situation or experience that confronts us. As one of my best friends Tanya Rieger would say, "Some people can't handle it when it's time to produce and represent." She and I often laugh and talk about this subject, and I believe she is right when she says, "Some people just cannot step up to the plate, Jermaine." Through research, I now understand a little better and a little clearer why some people (including me) cannot produce, represent, and step up to the plate at times—when we have a fear of success.

If we allow the fear of success to reign supreme in our lives, we will never know what we can fully become in life. Knowing the greatness of your talents, abilities, gifts, and skills is one of the surest ways to boost your self-concept and give back to the universe. You can actually bless and contribute to your generation when you tap into your human resources and celebrate them. Renowned psychologist Abraham Maslow coined this self-awareness as self-actualization. Self-actualization is the inborn drive to develop all one's talents and capabilities. It involves psychologically and emotionally understanding one's own potential as well as accepting others as unique individuals.

People with disadvantaged childhoods or unfortunate beginnings do become successful, of course, but they often do not enjoy what they have achieved because they do not feel they deserve it. Some people simply feel so guilty that they do not allow themselves to celebrate and honor the accomplishments and achievements they've made in life, school, & work.

# Barrier 9
# Fear of the Unknown

Have you ever wondered why people go to the same restaurant over and over again? Or why people pick the same dish over and over again, even though there are thirty other items on the menu to pick from? Or why people take the same route to work day after day, week after week, month after month, year after year when there are several other routes they might take? How about people who buy the same colognes, perfumes, and oils over and over again when there are thousands of other fragrances for them to purchase and choose?

Finally, how about those who think the same thoughts throughout their entire lives? They never challenge themselves or the validity of their thoughts and views. They never think outside of their normal thoughts, and they never open up their creative, innovative, and imaginative sides.

## Familiarity is safe

People keep doing what they are doing and keep getting what they are getting because it is safer to gravitate towards the familiar and easy. They avoid any situation or experience that is new and unfamiliar. If you change nothing, then nothing changes. If people want different results in their private, personal, or professional lives, they must be willing to change the way they have been doing things. They must be willing to do different things to get different results in life. People often complain about making changes in life, but they keep doing the same familiar things repeatedly.

> **Consider this mathematical problem**
> **2 + 3 = 5 and 3 + 2 = 5.**

No matter how you switch the variables around, your total will always be five. If you want a different total, then you have to change the variables in the equation. A familiar quote by an unknown author I have heard thousands of times and I totally agree with states, "Insanity is doing the same thing over and over but expecting different results."

If we obey our fear of the unknown, then we limit our opportunities to explore new horizons and to rise to new heights in life. If we follow the fear of the unknown, then we only do the comfortable, familiar, and safe things in life. When we step outside of our comfort zone, we discover what is really inside of us, which allows us to fully use and maximize our talents, abilities, gifts, and skills. A common characteristic of successful individuals is their ability to embrace and welcome risk-taking opportunities that will enhance all aspects of their lives.

## FEAR—False Evidence Appearing Real

When we fear the unknown, we fear something that is not even present; we are actually afraid of the invisible. When I was in high school, a very intelligent minister, named Elder Ellis Jones, told me that fear was an acronym that stood for False Evidence Appearing Real.

According to trial attorneys, when false evidence is presented in court, they attempt to have this false evidence disregarded, disqualified, and tossed out. Why can't we subscribe to the same philosophy? Why can't we disregard, disqualify, and throw out our fears, especially if the fears are unfounded? This answer lies in one word in this fear acronym—one word that prevents us from simply ignoring *any* and *all* false evidence—"appearing." Appearing means coming into view, becoming visible, seeming likely or real. In most people's minds, if it looks real, it is real. Guess what? It is real to them because people's perceptions are their realities. This is why the false evidence appearing real cannot be thrown out, disregarded, and disqualified. Everything we perceive as real through our five senses actually becomes real to us. This is very unfortunate because, in reality, not everything that *looks* real *is* real and if it appears real, people treat it as real (reality).

## Power of the unknown

The fear of the *unknown* is the fear of entering and embarking upon uncharted, unfamiliar, and unknown territory. This fear prevents people from taking risks, trying new things, and exploring new avenues in life. On the other hand, the *known* are things we have a previous knowledge of—things that provide predictability and comfort, things we have personal experience with, and things that are familiar to our daily experiences. The known is also anything we can perceive through the five senses: sight, sound, smell, taste, and touch. People's minds are especially secure with the known because the *known* is certain, comfortable, common, familiar, predictable, and individuals feel more confident and relaxed when they are functioning within known boundaries.

I believe the core reason people have a fear of the unknown is because they cannot control and predict the outcome of certain situations. This lack of control breeds feelings of anxiety, uncertainty, stress, and perceived helplessness. I believe this is the key factor that gives the fear of the unknown its power and strength. People feel extremely uneasy and uncomfortable when they do not know what to expect in a given situation—when they cannot see how something is going to turn out from start to finish. Yes, I know it can be very scary, stressful, and nerve-wracking when we do not know the outcome of a given situation. I also agree that the unknown is filled with uncertainty, vagueness, and mystery.

# Two strategies for confronting and overcoming the fear of the unknown

Here are two powerful strategies I use in my own life to confront and challenge my fear of the unknown.

**1.** ***"Proper preparation and practice prevent poor performance."***

This strategy is a concept borrowed from Bob Pike, CEO of a Minneapolis-based training company called Creative Techniques International. Mr. Pike believes the best way to get the desired results from a training session is to follow the advice in his quote.

Now, I am not sharing this information with you to prepare you to become a trainer like Mr. Pike. But through creative thinking and meditation, I took Mr. Pike's quote a step further and applied it to everyday life. See, I believe that if people properly prepare and practice, they can prevent their own poor performances in life, school, & work. While teaching public speaking over the last ten years, I have observed the number one reason why over 90 percent of my students perform horribly on their first two speeches: They are not prepared and have not rehearsed (practiced) for this new and unknown audience. Every audience is unknown, but if I do my homework and find out as much as I can about the audience before my presentation, research my topic, and practice my speech, I will put myself in the best position to significantly minimize my fear of the unknown.

Will you eliminate *all* poor performances in life? No. But by preparing, planning, and embracing the unexpected, you can significantly and greatly reduce negative performances. Yes, the unknown will confront you with situations you may not be ready for, such as untimely deaths, illnesses, divorces, breakups, or home/car repairs you cannot pay for, but if you begin to train yourself emotionally and mentally, you can be in the best possible position to handle your fear of the unknown when it presents itself.

2. *"The best way to predict the future, which of course is the unknown, is for you to create it."*

This strategy is from another philosophical quote, which says that *you* create your future, not your husband, not your wife, your boyfriend, girlfriend, grandmother, grandfather, aunt, uncle, or cousin. You must determine the course of your life by making wise choices. You must proactively create what you want to have in life, school, & work—you must make this happen. You create it. This is where goal planning and goal setting are essential.

You set your goals for life, school, & work, you make it happen, and you keep going until you have completed your task. You keep going, and don't you ever stop. Please do not stop getting what is yours in life, school, & work. And always keep in mind, if you do not take what is rightfully yours, someone else will.

## A special note to the reader:

There were two huge unknowns that happened to me while writing this book. My mom had a diabetic seizure, went into a coma for several months, had her leg amputated, and almost died. My younger brother was shot and killed while my mother was going through her personal challenges. My mother is still in a semi-comatose state, and she is not aware of the fact that she lost her youngest son. Even with all these unknown challenges that I didn't expect to happen like this, I still completed my dream and goal. I became the first author in my family. Question: are you willing to do the same for your dreams, goals, and aspirations? Don't allow the fear of the unknown to steal your dreams, goals, and aspirations.

# Barrier 10
## Procrastination

The tenth reason people do not set goals is because of the nasty evil spirit of procrastination. Every semester students in my courses learn about the nasty evil spirit of procrastination in a fun humorous way, but I always leave them with the negative consequences of developing such a dangerous habit. According to the book *The Complete Idiot's Guide To Breaking Bad Habits*, the word *procrastination* comes from the Latin verb *procrastinare*, which combines "pro," meaning "forward motion," and crastinus, meaning "belonging to tomorrow." This definition tells me procrastinators are willing to put off their actions until tomorrow when they can really put forth the effort today. I would personally like to define procrastination as the destructive and negative habit of putting things off until later.

Procrastination takes place when an individual fails to complete or follow through on a specific task within a certain time frame. It also involves deferring action or postponing tasks until the last minute. Procrastination is notorious for destroying lives and keeping people from living life to the fullest. People can procrastinate until they have blown, lost, or wasted an opportunity. Ask yourself, have you ever missed or blown an opportunity because of procrastination? How did missing out on a wonderful opportunity make you feel?

Procrastination can also have a negative impact on a person's character. An article by Joseph Ferrari, Ph.D., a professor of psychology at DePaul University in Chicago, in *Psychology Magazine* entitled, "How Do Students Cope with

Procrastination? They Lie," revealed that "College students admit that at least 70 percent of their excuses for missed assignments are lies." What was even more interesting to learn was that most instructors almost always accepted the students' excuses at face value, which reinforced and enabled students to continue to be chronic procrastinators and skillful liars.

## So, why do people procrastinate?

J.R. Ferrari and J.L. Johnson in their book *Procrastination and Task Avoidance* explain four reasons why people procrastinate due to faulty thinking. I will add personal examples for each reason:

1. **People believe they must "feel like" doing the task in order to complete the task or succeed at it.**

   ***Example:*** A person wants to lose weight, but they don't feel inspired to go to the gym or feel as excited about going as they did a few weeks ago. Remember, from hour to hour and week-to-week, our emotional states can change very quickly, so we must not rely on our emotions to dictate what actions we will take in life, school, or work. It is a myth to believe you have to feel like working out in order to work out.

   ***Note to reader:*** *As I sit here at my computer typing tonight, I really would like to be at a concert that I wanted to attend with my good friends. However, I remembered my priorities and my deadline, so I disciplined myself to stay at home to complete the book that you are currently reading.*

2. **People overestimate the amount of motivation they'll have in the future to complete the task.**

   ***Example:*** A student knows on the first day of class that they have to write a twelve-to-fifteen-page final paper at the end of the semester. The student thinks, "Oh well, I have sixteen weeks to write this paper." Each week the professor checks with the students to see how they are progressing on their papers and even encourages the students not to wait until the last moment because the assignment can be emotionally overwhelming if they attempt to do it all at once. The student passively listens in class, but calculates that he or she will set one entire week aside to work on the paper and that should suffice. Well, guess what? The student doesn't listen to the sound advice of the experienced professor, waits until the very last week of class, becomes overwhelmed with the work load, and can't complete the assignment on the expected due date. The student asks for an extension, and the professor says, "No I'm sorry; I can't grant you an extension. If I granted you an extension, I would need to extend that opportunity to all five hundred of my other students this semester."

3. *People overestimate the amount of time they have left to complete the task.*

   *Example:* Imagine that I am a caretaker of a medium size apartment complex, and I receive a free rent credit for cleaning vacant apartments each month. One of my major responsibilities is to have each apartment thoroughly cleaned and sanitized to advertise for potential renters. Well, it is the end of the month, and I have five families moving out on a Friday and seven potential renters coming on Monday morning to view the vacancies. I know that I should begin cleaning on Friday after the families move out to be prepared for a Monday morning showing of the available apartments. Well, I procrastinate and wait until Sunday afternoon, and as I enter each apartment, I discover each family lived like filthy pigs and never cleaned their apartment on a regular basis. I realize I have to do major cleaning in each apartment, and I will not be ready to show the apartments on Monday. Now, I have to call the potential renters to reschedule the showings, but they cannot reschedule because they need to find an apartment and move somewhere as soon as possible. They rent from my competitor two blocks away, and I miss several opportunities due to my own procrastination, which causes me to get fired for not meeting my job expectations and requirements in a timely manner.

### 4. People underestimate how long it will take to complete the task.

*Example:* Pete the profuse procrastinator was horrible at paying his bills on time. He spent much more money than he earned. Eventually, he had to file for bankruptcy because he lived above his means and had poor money management skills. When Pete filed for bankruptcy, he was allowed to keep his brand new vehicle with one huge stipulation—that his car payment be paid promptly on the seventh day of each month. He was told that if he could not make the payment, his brand new vehicle would be repossessed immediately without any notification.

Pete the profuse procrastinator did really well with paying his bills promptly for six months straight, but at the beginning of the seventh month, he had a few financial challenges, which forced him to make his car payment late—on the twelfth. Pete did not think five days would make a huge difference, but after three days of being late with his payment, when he left for work at 7:00 a.m., he realized his car was not parked in the parking space he had parked the previous night. Because it was a brand new car, Pete immediately called the police department to report it stolen. After sharing the situation with his older brother, who asked Pete if he had made his payment on time, it immediately struck Pete that he should check to see if his car had been repossessed. Sure enough, that's what had happened. His car had been repossessed. Why had this happened? Pete simply procrastinated by underestimating the amount of time he had. He really did not think they would really repossess his vehicle that quickly.

# Part 4:
## 8 Steps to Success & Making Your Goals Happen

In Part Three, you learned to identify barriers that prevented you from achieving your goals. In Part Four, You'll discover the eight steps to help you overcome those barriers by planning for and reaching each of your goals in life, school, & work.

# Step 1
## Clearly Identify What You Want & Know Why

When setting goals, it is really critical, and I mean *really critical*, that you fully understand what you want and why you want it. Setting clear goals is the first step to overcoming the problems of Barrier 4, or the idea that setting and achieving goals requires too much effort. When you are clear about your goals, you can easily visualize and fully understand what you are going after and attempting to accomplish. Crystal-clear goals leave no room for ambiguity or obscurity.

### Moving from abstract to clear goals

Here are a few examples of extremely abstract and unclear goals. Remember, when your goals are too abstract and unclear, you lack mental clarity and waste valuable time in the process of trying to pursue an unclear goal.

Let's say you want to make a *lot of money*. The term *lot* in this phrase is an example of abstract language, which is language that is vague and unclear when describing goals, events, ideas, or objects. To clarify this goal, you should determine how much money would be a lot to you or enough for the lifestyle you desire to live. Is it $50,000 a year? $100,000? Two million? Fifty million? Each person has a different perception of what *a lot of money* is.

## Classic statements from my workshops

I often hear people who value the traditional family structure say, "I want to become a better spouse and a better parent." First, I tell them to ask themselves: Better than what? Better than whom? What exactly do you want to make better? Do you want to listen more or express yourself more often with your spouse and children? Do you want to spend more quality time with them? You must first determine and identify the distinctive factors that will make you a better parent and a better spouse.

"I would like a good job when I graduate." How would you define a good job? Is a good job determined by money, location of the organization, the values of the organization, the culture and environment of the organization, benefits package, or chance for career advancement and upward mobility?

Some people say, "I just want to be happy in life." I usually respond with questions to challenge individuals to use more concrete descriptors for what they want out of life, school, & work rather than abstract language. What is happiness? What currently makes you happy? What factors in your life are making you unhappy? What steps need to be taken to eliminate negative factors from your life? Will eliminating those factors increase your level of happiness? Whatever you want out of life, school, & work, you must clearly identify what it is because only then can you achieve what you have designated as a clear and desirable goal.

## Try brainstorming

If you are not exactly sure what you want out of life, school, & work, spend a little time brainstorming. Brainstorming is an effective activity that helps you generate ideas with the ultimate objective of getting as many thoughts on paper as possible within a specific time frame.

Effective brainstorming consists of four components:

**1.** A quiet and distraction free environment.

**2.** Paper.

**3.** A pen (or your favorite writing instrument).

**4.** A stopwatch.

Before you begin brainstorming, you have to think about one goal or one area of your life or career you would like to work on and improve. Remember, you cannot brainstorm without having an idea or concept to work on. So sit down in a stress-free environment and decide what you really want to pursue. I believe identification of your goals enhances participation and dedication.

***Here is an example*** of how brainstorming can help generate ideas to help you clearly identify what you want.

Nyelah is a successful executive in corporate America where she has spent the last ten years of her life in sales, marketing, and management. However, she feels very unfulfilled and has lost her desire to maintain her career in corporate America. Psychologically, she visualizes starting her own business, working for herself, and creating a powerful and well respected, medium-sized company. The problem is that Nyelah does not know exactly what kind of business endeavor to pursue; therefore, her mentor encourages her to begin brainstorming for three to five minutes at a time on her entrepreneurial endeavors.

Nyelah finds a quiet space in her basement, grabs a legal pad, a green ball point pen, a fine tip pen at that, and begins to think about her work experience, talents/ skills set, and personal business interest. Each day she does a brainstorming activity where she sets her stopwatch for three minutes, she writes down all the possible businesses she could start based on her previous work experience, talents, acquired skills, and business interests.

On the third day, when she completes the brainstorming activity, Nyelah has generated thirty-seven potential business endeavors. From this initial list of thirty seven, she begins to narrow down what she wants to do and where she wants to focus her energy. Nyelah made a final decision that was totally driven by her values and what she believed to be the most viable ideas that could be turned into moneymaking businesses.

I firmly believe that if you are not clear about where you are going, you will most certainly get lost because you will take any available route, road, or street, even if it is the wrong one. You must clearly determine what you really want out of life, school, & work in order to avoid being thrown off course by indecisiveness and confusion.

## Create a clear path

It does not matter what you want out of life, school, or work; what matters is how clear and specific you are when defining your goals. Clearly identifying what you want saves a lot of time and energy because it gives you an ideal vision, or at least a good idea, of where you are going. Then you will be able to recognize it when you see it.

Successful goal achievers know precisely what they want, and they can describe their goals in vivid and colorful detail.

So take out time for yourself, and clearly identify exactly what you want from each of your goals.

# Step 2
## Perform a Needs Analysis: Knowledge, Skills, Desires, & Will

The second step to achieving your goals is to perform a *needs analysis*, which I define as taking a personal inventory of your knowledge, skills, desires, and will. I instruct all workshop participants to take a personal inventory of what they are capable of doing before they attempt to accomplish any goal. Taking inventory of what you need in order to accomplish your goals will help you overcome Barriers 6 through 9 by teaching you how to overcome your fears. It does not matter if the goal is small, medium, or large—minor or major. Performing a personal needs analysis is mandatory! It is a critical MUST!

**Needs analysis** A needs analysis is a thorough examination of the *knowledge, skills, desires, and will* needed to accomplish your goals. The needs analysis process is important because the goal is to help goal setters and achievers investigate what resources they currently have access to and what resources they will need in order to accomplish their goals. This analysis and process is extremely valuable because it allows goal setters and achievers to calculate the cost of their goals before they get started. This is a proactive approach to goal setting and achievement. It can prevent you from wasting time, money, and energy.

- **Knowledge** is investigating and finding specific information that addresses the question, "What do you need to know and do to accomplish a specific goal?" Knowledge is acquiring a full understanding of what lies ahead of you as you set out to fulfill your dreams, goals, and aspirations. An example of knowledge:

While a student at Elmhurst College, I started a business out of my dorm room called Jermaine's Cleaning Services. My goal was to earn extra income to assist with paying tuition and daily living expenses. Before I executed on the idea, I read many books about how to start a cleaning service business. I needed to know what challenges and potential problems I would face before I launched this business. On my quest for knowledge I learned many valuable things, such as the minimum investment required, proper and safe cleaning techniques, best practices, client contracts, fee setting, billing, promotions, and marketing.

- **Skill** is the ability to perform a task or a job. For each goal you want to achieve, there is a certain skill set and competency level you must have developed in order to accomplish that goal. Understanding the required skill set and competency level helps you understand what steps need to be taken to achieve your goals. Then your T.A.G.S. will determine what gets done—T.A.G.S. are your talents, abilities, gifts, and skills. In the case where you cannot personally perform the required tasks, you must be resourceful enough to find someone else who is capable.

*An example of skills:* I asked myself before I fully launched the business, "Jermaine, what cleaning skills do you currently possess, and what cleaning skills do you need to learn before you begin marketing and promoting your business to home owners and apartment complexes?" Fortunately, I was a very competent cleaner due to my mother, Carolyn Charmaine Davis. She valued a clean house, and she passed this value on to all of her children. So as a child, I grew up regularly mopping, waxing, sweeping, dusting, vacuuming, washing dishes, and scrubbing down walls and sanitizing toilets. I came to the table with marketable skills that I could immediately offer to my potential clients.

- **Desires** (emotional state) are strong feelings such as craving, wanting, and yearning for something badly enough that it compels you to take action. Your desires are the emotions and feelings you experience when you anticipate and think of your dreams, goals, and aspirations.

  *An example of desire:* My desire to start Jermaine's Cleaning Services wasn't because I was passionate about cleaning up other people's messes and filth. I had a huge desire to be in control of my own destiny, work schedule, and financial status. I knew that starting my own business would allow me these privileges. I was driven by the spirits of capitalism and entrepreneurialism. When I started the business, my friends were making between $4.25 and $6.00 per hour as college students, and I was making between $15.00 to $30.00 per hour depending on the fee I negotiated for each cleaning contract.

- **Will** (mental state) is the conscious and mental commitment and dedication you need in order to make sure you accomplish and fulfill your dreams, goals, and aspirations. Will is having the mental drive, fortitude, and stamina to keep following and pursuing your goals even when your situation looks bleak and dark. A strong will keeps you going even when you don't feel like it. Unlike desire, which focuses on emotional strength, will focuses on mental strength, training, toughness, and conditioning.

  *An example of will:* I was mentally ready and determined to succeed at this business. I had braced myself for being rejected. I had learned in my sales and marketing class that it took one hundred sales calls to get ten sales presentations, and out of the ten sales presentations, you would get one new client. Call me stubborn, hardheaded, or idealistic, but for some reason, I did not believe my journey would be that difficult. Don't get me wrong. I knew there would be challenges and work involved, but I was ready and determined to succeed.

I remember I arose one Saturday morning, and I wrote down all of my ideas on a yellow legal pad. I went to the computer lab and typed up a flyer introducing Jermaine's Cleaning services to the city of Elmhurst within walking distance of the college. I remember one of the marketing tag lines on the flyer was, "Jermaine is ready, willing, and able to do the jobs, grunt work, and house chores your kids refuse to do." I made approximately two hundred flyers and began distributing them around the city of Elmhurst. I had no car or bike at the time, so I traveled on foot knocking on doors, introducing myself to potential clients, and leaving flyers in mailboxes. I hung flyers at local grocery stores; I left them at bus stops, on message boards, or at any visible location where people would see my services. This project took about five to six hours that Saturday morning and afternoon. I can vividly remember being extremely exhausted with aching feet that particular day. I was determined to make it happen, and I refused to stop and give up, even when my negative self-talk was telling me, "Jermaine, you're stupid. No one is going to hire you. Your flyers are going straight to the trash can." These were the thoughts I had as I went from house to house, but I kept going because I was mentally ready and determined to succeed.

Now the good news was that when I arrived back at my dorm room, I had three homeowners ready to use my services. I started the next day with a married couple (a retired scientist and a social worker,) Mr. and Mrs. Millar. When business would get slow, I would call my clients and negotiate deals with them. I leveraged referrals as a business strategy and tactic. I told my clients that if they would refer me to local family members and friends, I would give them a 50 percent discount off their next cleaning job. I was always thinking ahead and mentally preparing myself to expect the unexpected by asking myself what would I do if an unfortunate situation happened, and then I would devise a plan to overcome that particular barrier or obstacle.

The key to an effective needs analysis is to address all four of these components—knowledge, skills, desires, and will—or the goal cannot be achieved. I think of it as a form of strategic planning to prevent creating unnecessary headaches and wasting valuable time. One example of a group that finds this method useful includes athletic coaches who perform needs analyses to plan for successful winning seasons.

## My personal needs analysis process

I used the needs analysis process when I decided to produce my first audio book. To begin, I made a list of the knowledge required to complete this tedious, time-consuming, and emotionally draining task. Due to the many research papers and theses I had written while in graduate school, the writing aspect was not my greatest problem. However, I lacked a great deal of knowledge in the areas of editing, artwork, cover design, marketing, promotions, copyright laws, and other important information. To compensate, I took a fabulous course offered by a very knowledgeable woman, Patricia J. Bell, author of *Roughing It Elegantly*. For $49 for a ten-hour, three-week course, I benefited tremendously from Patricia's years of expertise as her knowledge became my knowledge. During this process, I learned that it was wise and okay to leverage the knowledge of those who were more knowledgeable and experienced than I was. I had to assess the skills I already possessed and the skills I was lacking, which revealed what I needed to develop in order to fulfill my dream of producing my first audio book. After taking the class, it was quite evident that producing an audio book was not for the insecure, feeble, undisciplined, or easily distracted. I knew it was not going to be easy, but the rewards would be both exhilarating and invigorating.

After my assessment, I made up my mind that nothing was going to stand in the way of me producing my first audio book;

I was willing to do whatever it took. I was willing to fund this project with my life's savings. I worked extra jobs, I took classes, I purchased books, and I said no a lot to friends, family members, and colleagues to avoid procrastinating and falling behind schedule. I was not going to allow any form of adversity or discouragement to stand in my way.

For many hours, days, weeks, and months, I sat at Barnes & Noble, read on my living room floor or at my computer desk, wrote, hoped, and prayed that my words, stories, and examples would help my listeners elevate to the next level in their lives and careers. This was the passion and catalyst that drove my motivation; it gave me the drive to keep going at times when I felt like throwing in the towel and quitting.

### *Personal motives:*

Believe it or not, I did not write *this* book just for me or to stroke my own ego. I wrote this book for my fifteen year-old sister, Katrina; my twenty-one-year-old brother, Greg (who tragically passed during the course of writing this book); my smiling mother, Charmaine; and my thought-provoking grand-mother, Margaret Ann Davis. I also wrote this book for all the men and women in my childhood neighborhood who did not make it and for those who fell victim to gangs, drug abuse, ille-gal drug sales, prison, alcoholism, prostitution, street hustlin', and street violence. I also wrote this book for you.

So I ask you, are you truly motivated enough to make your dreams happen? If so, remember that a needs analysis is an absolute necessity—take inventory of the knowledge, skill set, desire (emotional state), and will (mental state) required to accomplish each of your goals. This needs analysis will give you a solid base to start from.

# Step 3
# Write Down All Barriers & Obstacles

The third step in realizing your goals is that you must write down all potential barriers and challenges that may stand in the way of you accomplishing your goals. Writing down all the things that might stand in your way is an excellent way to decrease the fear of failure that is outlined in Barrier 6. This process is referred to as *proactive planning*—pre-planning before a negative event or situation actually happens. It requires having a game plan in place before chaos or a crisis occurs. The opposite of this is *reactive planning*—not having a game plan in place prior to disasters.

I teach at a college where many of the students are non-traditional, typically older in age, adults with families and adults who also work either part-time or full-time. They have various reasons behind their decisions to attend college. Their reasons include career advancement opportunities, upgrading or learning a new skill, obtaining a degree or completing a previously unfinished degree, or merely attempting to receive a higher salary by taking educational and managerial classes.

Of course, I applaud this effort, but it never ceases to amaze me how many individuals register for courses without taking into account how much time, work, and commitment it takes to successfully complete a course or even an entire degree. Certain students never consider the challenges of being a committed student, dedicated employee, and devoted friend and family member all at once.

## Compromise and sacrifice
## (You must give up to go up)

This is where compromise, negotiation, and sacrifice play enormous roles in the goal setting and achieving process. You must be willing to give up in order to go up. We all get 168 hours a week—no more, no less. When attempting to accomplish certain goals, you have to be willing to give up certain activities to make room and time for other priorities that demand immediate attention. Your personal and professional values will determine where you spend your time and energy. People must be willing to stay focused on the goal at hand and dedicate a portion of their weekly 168 to breathing life into their personal and professional dreams and goals. Dr. Stephen R. Covey, Roger Merrill, and Rebecca Merrill in their book, *First Things Firsts*, share a simple idea to keep people focused on the goal at hand and that idea is to understand, "The Main Thing is to Keep the Main Thing the Main Thing." Everyone must determine what matters most to him or her. Each person must ask himself or herself what he or she is temporarily, or even permanently, willing to give up in his or her present lifestyle in order to achieve their goals in the future.

I can personally tell what a person values by how they regularly prioritize the important activities in their life and how they manage and use their time. The amount of time and energy people devote to their goals will determine how far they go in life, school, & work. I have seen some students suffer a complete mental, emotional, and physical breakdown because they are overwhelmed by multiple obligations—family, friends, work, and school—all competing for the same time and energy. Remember, something has to give at times in order to succeed.

### People don't plan to fail—they fail to plan

One of the main reasons this happens is that they failed to plan properly. They did not plan proactively; their actions and behaviors were reactive. They did not write down all the potential barriers, challenges, and obstacles. They did not go through the process of determining how much time and energy would be needed to complete each task or obligation. As students, they failed to think about homework, group projects, reading time, study time, writing time, lab time, and thinking time for each topic or class. Some never took into account the drive time or the expenses for gas, books, school supplies, food, childcare, and travel.

Keep in mind that no matter what type of goal you set, you must calculate the cost, level of commitment, dedication, and devotion you must have in order to achieve the goal. I suggest that people calculate the cost of each of their goals and ask themselves if they are willing to pay the cost of accomplishing that particular life, school, or career goal.

Please, I repeat, please write down all potential barriers, challenges, and obstacles that you may encounter. **Then plan accordingly**. Strategic planning can and will significantly reduce these challenges, preventing them from overwhelming you mentally, emotionally, and physically. You won't eliminate and eradicate all of your problems, but following this step will prepare you for the unexpected.

# Step 4
## Develop a "Dream Team"

The fourth step in the goal setting and achieving process is that you need to develop a powerful "Dream Team." Your Dream Team is made up of a cast of dedicated and supportive members—a lineup of all your favorite number-one draft picks in life—individuals you admire, respect, trust, and value. The purpose of your Dream Team is to help you succeed and attain victory while providing support to you as you strive to reach your goals. They assist you on your journey as you set out to accomplish your goals in life, school, & work.

## Surround yourself with diverse, intelligent, and successful people

Developing a Dream Team means bringing together inventive, imaginative, and resourceful people who know more than you do, who are a step ahead of you, and who can point you in the right direction. A great way to overcome a low self-concept, fear of rejection, or fear of the unknown mentioned in Barriers 5, 7, and 9 is to develop a Dream Team. You want to pick people who are diverse in every sense of the word. Actually, the more diverse the Dream Team members are, the better it is for you. By diverse, I mean diversity beyond culture, gender, and race. I mean really select individuals who are diverse perceptually, ideologically, and philosophically because their diverse insights will introduce you to new concepts and ideas you probably would have never considered. No successful person gets anywhere alone. Do not feel threatened by people who are smarter, more intelligent, and more talented than you are. Their talent only helps you.

### Examples of successful people:

Media and fashion mogul Russell Simmons is the creator and owner of the highly successful hip-hop clothing line *Phat Fashions*, which consists of Phat Farm, Baby Phat, and Phat Farm Kids whose 2003 sales are estimated at $615 million. Simmons states, "Everybody around me is smarter than me." His entertainment ventures have consisted of successful projects such as Def Comedy Jam and the recent Def Poetry Jam series. Finally, in 1985, Russell Simmons co-founded Def Jam Records, which featured famous hip-hop artists such as LL Cool J, the Beastie Boys, Public Enemy, Jay-Z, Ludacris, Red Man, Method Man, and many others.

One of Russell Simmon's good friends, billionaire Donald J. Trump, real estate titan, best-selling author, and mega-superstar of the successful TV series, *The Apprentice,* says in his book *How to Get Rich*, "You need competent people with an inherent work ethic. I'm not a complacent person and I can't have a complacent staff. I move forward quickly and so they must."

Those who are intellectually superior to him do not threaten even the richest man in the world, Bill Gates, whose personal wealth is $46 billion. In the book *The Bill Gates Way,* he states, "I'd have to say my best business decisions have had to do with picking people. I don't hire bozos." Bill Gates hires the best talent for his organization. It has been said that his company, Microsoft, only hires the top 1 percent of graduates who have excelled within their fields.

One of the quickest and surest ways to gradually stop personal and organizational growth and development is to become overtaken by envy, jealousy, and an over-inflated ego. Those who operate from a scarcity mentality believe that there is only a limited amount of resources in life, school, & work. This way of thinking and processing is notorious for breeding outlandish behaviors where individuals become overly threat-ened and fearful of those who are more accomplished, compe-tent, and intelligent. Those who operate from the scarcity premise will sometimes refuse to hire and promote individuals who are more accomplished, competent, and intelligent than themselves; some will even go to great lengths to find ways to eliminate positions or simply fire these individuals.

The opposite of the scarcity mentality is the abundance mentality. Those who operate from an abundance mental-ity believe that there are enough resources for everyone in life, school, & work. They truly believe there is enough pie for every-one to eat from in life. These individuals recognize and under-stand that the Creator has freely given T.A.G.S. (talents, abilities, gifts, and skills) to each person on planet Earth. Great intel-ligence or talents do not threaten them. They actually embrace, respect, and welcome those who develop their T.A.G.S. Those with an abundance mentality become inspired and motivated by watching and observing talented people in action. They believe that iron sharpens iron and the only way to become excellent within their chosen field is to surround themselves with greatness and excellence. They know the only way to grow a successful enterprise is to hire intelligent and competent employees. Author and business writer, Dennis Kimbroy PhD. states, "If you're the smartest person on your team, then you need to get another team." Almost all great and successful individuals embrace the abundance mentality. This mentality is necessary for creating a successful and competent Dream Team.

## Be wary of dream stealers

You should select your Dream Team very, very carefully. In the process of picking and choosing, proceed with extreme caution. Be analytical, meticulous, and objective when evaluat-ing those with whom you will share your dreams, goals, and aspirations. Why should you be so careful? Because planet Earth is full of individuals whom I call "professional dreamshatterers." Les Brown, motivational speaker and author of the book *Live Your Dreams*, calls them "dream-stealers."

Dr. Shad Helstetter, author of the book *The Self-Talk Solution*, says, "…as much as 77 percent of everything we think is negative…." People's perceptions of themselves—their self-concept and their esteem level—greatly influence how they see the world and the type of advice and feedback they give to others. Many studies reveal that varying esteem levels can have a powerful effect on the way we engage and interact with others. In their book *Looking Out, Looking In*, Ronald Adler, Neil Towne, & Russell Proctor support this belief. "Sometimes this low self-esteem is manifested in hostility toward others because the communicator takes the approach that the only way to look good is to put others down." Adler, Towne, & Proctor suggest that people with high self-esteem are more likely to think positively and well of others, but people with low self-esteem are likely to disapprove of others, and they feel especially threatened and insecure around others they view as better, more accomplished, or superior in some way. This explains why you have to be extremely careful when sharing your dreams and goals. Due to inaccurate thinking, some people will rain on your parade if they have no parade to be a part of or if they dislike parades all together. They have become conditioned to a pessimistic way of thinking.

No matter how simple or detailed you are in explaining your goals and dreams, some people will just not envision your dreams and goals as you envision them. Unfortunately, there will be times when you can't share your dreams and goals with those you love or who love you the most. You would think that our spouses, significant others, family members, and friends would automatically provide us with the greatest encouragement and support in all of our endeavors, but this is not true in all cases. Sometimes these individuals are the most negative and discouraging of all. Because we love, respect, and value them, and their opinions are most important to us, these individuals can be great barriers to success. Yes, well-meaning family members and friends can interfere with your success when they bombard you with negative energy that drains and kills your dreams and motivation.

### Protect your dreams

To avoid the negative criticism, cynicism, and pessimism of others, carefully select a Dream Team of members who want to see you succeed and win in the game of life. Remember to protect your dreams, goals, and aspirations as you would protect a precious child. You would not expose your precious child to just anyone or to everyone, so do not expose and reveal your dreams and goals to just anyone or to everyone.

# Step 5
# Ideas + Paper + A Pen = Written Goals

Do me a huge favor and take out a pen and several pieces of paper. The fifth step in achieving your goals is this formula: Ideas plus paper plus a pen equals written goals. In his book *Universal Laws of Success,* Brian Tracy states, "All successful people think on paper." In Part 3, you saw that Barrier 3 is not knowing how to set goals. Writing down your goals is one of the most important steps in learning how to set goals. Out of the many steps I have described in this book so far, all are extremely important, but I deeply believe that writing your goals down is one of the most vital components in the goal-achieving process. Dr. Shad Helmstetter, author of numerous self-help audio books and the book *Who Are You Really And What Do You Want?,* says, "It doesn't make any difference how important your idea is. If you say you have a goal, but then do not write it down—along with a simple action plan to reach it—your chances of actually reaching that goal are extremely low. (Studies have shown that when a goal is *not* written down, your chances of reaching that goal are somewhere between 3 percent and 7 percent. Not very good. But the moment you write the goal down, along with a simple plan to reach it, your chances of reaching the goal increase to as much as 70 or 80 percent.)"

## Documented research on written goals and success

In 1953, Yale University conducted a study to measure the rate of success for its graduating seniors. They wanted to know if goal setting was a prerequisite for success. The researchers wanted to know what percentage of the graduating seniors had identified specific goals for their careers and lives after college. The study revealed that only 3 percent of these seniors had set their goals properly by writing them down and clearly identifying what they wanted. Ten percent attempted to articulate and write down their goals, but they were unsure of them and, therefore, unfocused. Eighty-seven percent did not set any goals at all!

Twenty years later, Yale University concluded the study by interviewing the surviving members of the graduating class of 1953. The 3 percent who had properly set their goals accomplished more in financial wealth and career advancement than the other 97 percent combined. Astonishing!

As you can see, according to Dr. Shad Helmstetter's statistical research and Yale University's longitudinal study, writing your goals down and documenting them properly is one of the keys to goal setting and goal achievement. Although this information has been available for years, according to leading business writers, success researchers, and motivational speakers, only a small percentage of the U.S. population actually writes their goals down on paper.

- Brian Tracy, author of the book *Maximum Achievement*, has done research that reveals that less than 1 percent of the population actually writes down their goals.

- Dr. Shad Helmstetter states that only 2.78 percent of the population actually write down their goals.

- Zig Ziglar, in his audio book series *GOALS: How to Set Them and How to Reach Them,* asserts that only 3 percent of the population write down their goals.

- Dr. Denis Waitley, in his book *The New Dynamics of Goal Setting*, states, "Less than 5 percent of the U.S. population will ever write down a goal that they want to achieve."

Whether it is 1, 3, or 5 percent, we can conclude that only a very, very small percentage of the population will ever write a goal down on paper. According to this research, people have between a 3 to 7 percent chance of reaching their goals if they do not write them down. Wow! Those odds are small. However, remember what Dr. Shad Helmstetter found in his research. We can increase our success rate to 70 or 80 percent when we write our goals down accompanied by a simple action plan.

Have you ever gone to the grocery store with a mental list rather than a written list only to find on your way home that you forgot the ketchup, bread, the salad dressing, and, of course, the Sunday newspaper? You could have avoided this hassle if only you had written down your needed items, which were your goals for your shopping excursion.

Daydreaming, wishing, and thinking without a concrete game plan recorded on paper will not help you reach and achieve your goals—all successful people think on paper.

## Steps to become part of your goals on a daily basis

**First,** writing your goals down on paper allows you to see your goals and plans on a regular basis. The key is repetition, repetition, and more repetition. It has been said that repetition is the mother of skill. The more you see your goals on paper, the more you become acquainted and familiar with them, and the more you become a *part* of them and eventually fully invested in them.

**Second,** you should review your goals daily, weekly, and monthly. The more you review your written goals on paper, the more your goals enter into your short-term memory and eventually into your long-term memory. If your goals are only stored in your short-term memory, then you limit yourself to only achieving goals that you can recall within thirty seconds. This becomes even more of a challenge for those who have a difficult time with remembering and recalling information. The book *Psychology in Action* states, "Short term memory is memory containing things a person is presently thinking about and having a capacity limited to about seven items and duration of about thirty seconds." Because our lives and minds are already full due to life issues, constant message overload, and daily preoccupation with life, school and/or our careers, it is in our best interests to write our goals down on paper. Writing them down will increase the probability of remembering what matters most to us.

In their book *Looking Out, Looking In,* Adler, Towne, & Proctor state, "Research suggests that most people remember only about 50 percent of what they hear immediately after hearing it. Within eight hours, the 50 percent remembered drops to about 35 percent. After two months, the average recall is only about 25 percent of the original message." Short-term memory is designed to be a temporary place where information is briefly stored and processed for limited retrieval. This important piece of research really reinforces the purpose of writing goals down on paper because writing goals down helps to prevent us from losing 75 percent of an important goal after two months. Remember, our goal is to accomplish our goal. If we forget about our goals we can never accomplish them.

**Third,** transfer your goals from short-term memory to long-term memory. I believe this can be achieved by involving as many of the five senses (sight, sound, smell, taste, and touch) into the goal setting and goal achieving process as possible. The goal is to get your whole entire being and body into the process while you are creating and pursuing your goals. When you write your goals down on paper and review them routinely, you involve the senses of sight and touch, and while you are writing your goals down, you are moving them from short-term memory to long-term memory.

I also advocate talking about your goals as much as possible with your dream team and like-minded individuals. The more you hear your goals and get constructive advice and feedback, the more easily you move them from short-term to long-term memory. When individuals store information in their memories, it is never lost or forgotten. The problem lies in our inability to find the information when we need it. Dave Ellis in his book *Becoming a Master Student* states, "Brain research suggests that thoughts could wear paths in the memory. These paths are called neural traces. The more well worn the neural trace, the easier it is to retrieve [find] the thought. The more often you recall information, and the more often you put the same information into your memory, the easier it is to find." In other words, think, eat, and live your goals in your mind, body, soul, and spirit until you have achieved them. Unlike short-term memory, long-term memory does not have a limited space for storage or a time limit because this is where information, including goals and dreams, are stored permanently.

In his book *Silent Messages*, communications scholar, theorist, and researcher, Dr. Albert Mehrabian states that if individuals were exposed only once to an idea or concept, at the end of thirty days, they would remember less than 10 percent of that concept. But if they were exposed to the same idea or concept six times at intervals within those thirty days, they will retain more than 90 percent of the information. Exposure to your dreams and goals regularly and routinely is the key to achieving them. This means developing a good habit of reviewing your goals daily or, at a minimum, weekly. I suggest you regularly meet with your Dream Team as often as you can to involve them in the process of helping you to stay focused and on task.

I trust you fully understand how important it is to write down your goals and to review them as often as possible—that is, if you are serious about achieving your goals and making your dreams become realities.

# Step 6
# Create a Roadmap for Directions

The sixth step in achieving your goals is that you must create a road map to get you where you are going. Your roadmap is a carefully designed, charted out, step-by-step plan to guide and direct you from start to finish in the goal achieving process. Your road map provides you with a daily, weekly, and monthly blueprint as you move closer to achieving your goals. Your roadmap should be both concrete and visible, which will help you overcome Barrier 9: Fear of the Unknown.

## A roadmap analogy

A personal example of following a roadmap is my experience when I travel to a college or business for a presentation. When asked to speak at an organization, I religiously use the services of Mapquest.com, and I type into the software program my home or departing address and the address of the destination where I will be speaking. Within seconds, Mapquest.com provides me with a map and a text description of the best route to reach my destination, and to top it off, Mapquest.com even tells me the number of miles for the trip, and it gives me an approximate arrival time.

This concept is quite parallel to achieving your goals in life, school, & work. You must know where you are going, step-by-step, and how you plan to get there. I remember a song by a recording artist named Guru, a song that my college roommates and I really enjoyed. I am not sure they if really processed and internalized the lyrics as personally as I did, but we all liked the song's catchy, sing-along chorus which repeatedly instructed the fans and listeners to know exactly where they are headed while on the road to pursuing their dreams. If you do not know where you are headed, you will surely get lost or derailed, costing valuable time, money, and resources.

I've always believed that many more goals and dreams would be fulfilled universally if people would develop and follow a step-by-step action plan for each one of their goals. However, most people do not plan for success; they hope that somehow success will come looking for them and find them. There is only a small percentage of people who actually achieve success this way. Just as all great structures and monuments began with blueprints to follow, successful people have a game plan, they have blueprints to follow similar to architects and builders. Remember that no builder builds without blueprints to follow, and no goal achiever pursues goals without a roadmap to follow.

## Key questions to ask yourself

After you have clearly identified what you want out of life, school, & work and as you begin to create a plan and diagram for how you are going to accomplish each one of your goals, you should ask yourself three questions to help you stay focused and on task.

- What do I need to do on a daily basis to bring me closer to achieving my goals?
- How much work do I need to do weekly?
- What should I be doing monthly?

## Andrae's daily, monthly, and yearly roadmaps

R. Andraé Dobbey is founder and president of BrightLine Communications in Jacksonville, Florida. He is responsible for managing a retail office of seven sales associates, handling customer complaints and concerns, employee training, new business development, increasing annual sales by 10 percent, and personally selling $120,000 annually in cellular phones. At the end of the year, Andrae' reviews his major responsibilities and begins to plan for the new year. One of his main concerns is meeting his annual $120,000 sales goal. As he begins to develop a sketch of how he will accomplish this goal, he breaks this goal down incrementally. He wants to know exactly how many cell phones he needs to sell each day to meet his year-end goal. He breaks the figure down monthly by dividing $120,000 by twelve months and discovers he has to sell $10,000 a month in cellular phone sales. He breaks it down further into a weekly dollar amount by dividing $10,000 by four weeks, and now he has a weekly goal of $2,500 in phone sales. He works five days a week, so he breaks that down further by dividing $2,500 by five, and he reaches his daily sales figure of $500 a day. The average cellular phone in Andrae's store retails for $100, so he now understands that he must sell five cellular phones a day at a minimum of $100 per sale to reach his annual goal of $120,000. If he desired, Andrae' could even go a step further to see how many cellular phones he needs to sell each hour while he is at work to help him meet his year-end goals.

# Step 7
# Deadlines = Maximum Productivity

The seventh step to achieving your goals is setting deadlines for yourself. Deadlines equal maximum productivity, and all goals must be accompanied by deadlines. Setting deadlines is the single most effective way to overcome Barrier 10: Procrastination.

## Deadlines defined

For the purposes of this book, I define a deadline as a self-imposed measuring tool that will help you track your progress on your journey to achieving your goals. If you do not set deadlines for your goals, there is a very high probability you will blow off your goals whenever you feel you can replace them with something more immediately gratifying and satisfying. If you have goals without deadlines, you will be more apt to procrastinate when you should be working. You will waste more time, make more excuses, procrastinate more, and, as my older brother Russel Andrae' likes to say, *"lollygag more."* If you set a deadline, you will not be as likely to lollygag because deadlines allow us and force us to measure our progress. Then as we analyze our progress reports, we can make wise, informed decisions about what our next steps should be. During this process, we can also make new discoveries that enable us to make changes, such as adding to or deleting certain elements from our goals.

### *Decide on an exact date when setting deadlines*

Saying that you want to accomplish something next week, next month, next year, or before you die does not involve you intimately with your goals because you have not yet made a concrete commitment to them. When you have a commitment to a specific deadline, you know, consciously and subconsciously, that you must produce results by an actual date, as opposed to some intangible or abstract week, month, year, or decade. A few examples of abstract goals:

- I'll start school next year.
- I plan on registering for classes soon.
- I'll send out my resume and cover-letter within the next few weeks.
- I'll get in contact with you soon.
- My goal is to do my taxes sometime this month.

## Four ways deadlines can work for you

While writing this book, I discovered four benefits of having a specific deadline and definite due date in place.

### 1. *Saying no. Having a deadline gave me the strength and courage to say no.*

*My example:* I vividly remember one Thursday afternoon when I was sitting in my front room working on a difficult chapter in my book and experiencing a severe case of writer's block. My good friend and former college roommate, Rico, dropped by unexpectedly and looked at me with a peculiar expression of dismay. It was about ninety degrees outside, and the sun was shining beautifully, but my blinds were closed, my air conditioner was off, and I was sitting at my desk attempting to complete section one of the book. Rico reminded me that we live in Minnesota where the summer season weather is very unpredictable at times.

He said to me, "Man, what are you doing inside on a day like this? It is beautiful outside. Let's go for a drive to the lake and Dairy Queen, for cold refreshing treats. Let's go and enjoy this beautiful weather."

Now, I will admit I was very tempted—no *extremely* tempted—to stop writing and just blow off the rest of the day. But I had the strength and courage to say no because I had a deadline. Saying yes to Rico's request would have only postponed my progress and project.

Disappointed, Rico said, "Man, you're crazy." I looked back at him from my stuffy room in my dingy T-shirt and nylon sweats, and I said over and over, "June 8$^{th}$, June 8$^{th}$, June 8$^{th}$, man. June 8$^{th}$. I have a deadline." I told him I had made a commitment to my project and myself to finish writing section three by a specific date.

Rico laughed as he left my place and closed the door behind him. Yes, I had thoughts of giving in. I mean, who wouldn't want to feel that cool breeze from the Land of 10,000 Lakes, as Minnesota is often described, and have a cold, refreshing pecan cluster from Dairy Queen? But, as Rico left, I said, "Peace and good-bye," and I was able to turn down all that instant gratification with true peace and comfort because I had a deadline in mind, and I had responsibilities to stick to.

## 2. *Deadlines significantly reduce procrastination.*

Deadlines are designed to increase personal account-ability, productivity, and responsibility. If followed precisely, deadlines will accelerate your progress toward your goals. However, this greatly depends on how deter-mined, disciplined, and motivated you are towards accomplishing your goals.

*My example:* Honestly, I should have completed my previous publication, an audio book, in the summer of 1998. I did not complete it at that time because I procrastinated terribly. I was not disciplined enough, and, initially, I was not committed to a specific date for the completion of the audio book. At the time, I believed that finishing my audio book sometime in the summer of 1998 was a specific and clear enough deadline, but I was completely wrong. I had passed up an opportunity to teach summer school, which would have provided extra income. I forfeited this opportunity because my goals were to fully commit and dedicate myself to writing, reading, recording, and researching for the purpose of producing the audio book. My summer break lasted approximately twelve weeks, and I enjoyed each and every one of those twelve weeks by replacing my audio-recording responsibilities with more immediately gratifying activities, such as going out to eat with friends, watching television, shopping at the mall, talking on the telephone, surfing the Internet, playing basketball, and, of course, sleeping—simply being non-productive all day long.

See the deadline—the summer of 1998—was too big, too broad, too abstract, too intangible, and too vague for a realistic goal. I had not committed myself to an exact or definite date of completion; I had no specific date to be accountable to or responsible for. Therefore, it was too easy to justify my non-productive work habits because the deadline, the summer of 1998, allowed me a certain comfort, cushion, and flexibility I did not need. In May, I kept saying "I'll work on the book in June," but before I knew it, June was over, and I postponed the project until July. When July was over, I said "I'll work on the book in August," and before I knew it, September came, and it was time to start teaching again. I took the entire summer off to work on a book I never even started.

After that summer, I began setting a deadline for each of my goals, which made me both accountable and responsible. My deadlines became daily reminders of the work I needed to complete and the goals I wanted to accomplish.

### 3. *Prevent the Superman-and-Wonder-Woman Syndrome.*

Deadlines should prevent a bad habit I call the Superman-and-Wonder-Woman Syndrome. Individuals who suffer from this syndrome tend to overextend themselves by accepting and volunteering to do more than they can handle in life, school, & work. They take on more than they can juggle to win the social approval of others.

Remember that your deadlines are there to remind you of the commitments you have made to accomplishing your dreams and goals. To avoid the Superman-and-Wonder-Woman Syndrome, you must learn to say no without feeling guilty. It is okay to say, "I'm sorry, I would love to assist you on this project, but right now, I have prior obligations that demand my immediate attention." If you are committed to your goals, you must not play the game of telling people what they want to hear so you can win their favor and approval. Don't give in or commit to a request because you don't want to hurt their feelings. In the long run, you will gain more respect and credibility by being truthful and up front in the beginning rather than letting people down later because you didn't follow through on your word and commitment. Breaking a promise and not following through on your word really diminishes your credibility and believability.

I believe relationships are severely damaged when people do not keep promises and commitments. Therefore, it is important to understand that when you make a promise, people develop a hope and an expectation of that promise. They begin to look forward to the fulfillment of your words, so you must be true to your word if you want to be respected and embraced by others.

### 4. *Turn off your phones.*

Deadlines should make you turn off your telephone ringer and forward all calls to your voice mail at certain times. I attended one of Dr. Stephen R. Covey's seminars "First Things First," and at the seminar I heard an eye opening statistic, "When people are interrupted by others, it takes **seven minutes** for them to get back on track and task again."

**Seven minutes adds up.** It may not seem like a lot of time to you. However, six, seven, eight, or nine interruptions will put you far behind schedule. I actually believe people take more than seven minutes to get back on task after being interrupted. I do not have any research to support this hypothesis, but here is my reasoning: When individuals are involved in a project, they are involved physically, emotionally, and mentally. After attending to the interruption, you may restart the project physically, but you must also regain your concentration, focus, and momentum. It takes time to get back into the flow of things and to reconnect with the emotional and mental position you had prior the interruption.

So if you want to maximize your productivity, turn off that telephone and forward all calls to voice mail for a specified amount of time.

# Step 8
## Be Egotistical

The eighth step in achieving your goals is that you must learn to become egotistical. Now, I am not a comedian, and this is not a joke. Yes, you must be egotistical. The term *egotistical* has an extremely negative connotation in our society, but I believe there are times when we are in pursuit of our goals and dreams that we must be fully preoccupied with our personal achievements and interests. Once denounced and underrated, multi-platinum artist, songwriter, and producer Kanye West spoke about how important it was for him to have an ego to fuel his dream of breaking into an overcrowded and saturated music business. Mr. West says, "Now, I can let these dream killers kill my self-esteem or use my arrogance (ego) as esteem to power my dreams." I believe we must be sold out, relentlessly focused, and committed to our dreams, goals, and aspirations if we really want them to happen. Understanding this step to success helps individuals overcome the fears of failure, rejection, and success outlined in Barriers 6, 7, and 8. No one else is going to care about your dreams, goals, and aspirations more than you do; they are not supposed to because these are your dreams, goals, and aspirations, not theirs. Billionaire Donald Trump in his book *How to Get Rich* says about having an ego, "Having a well-developed ego, contrary to popular opinion, is a positive attribute. It is the center of our consciousness and serves to give us a sense of purpose. I remember saying to someone, 'Show me someone with no ego and I'll show you a big loser.'" Trump believes that having a positive ego is a prerequisite for success, especially for financial success. A healthy ego gives you the support to pursue and believe in your dreams, goals, and aspirations when others don't believe in you.

## My egotistical experience:

Recently I shared a business goal that I had with a few close friends and family members whom I care a lot about and trust. They all embraced the idea and applauded me on the idea, and the common denominator as far as their responses was, "That's the one Jermaine, that's the one." By "That's the one…," they were referring to the one idea that would be my break-though idea towards financial freedom and independence. Immediately, they all began to say, "Please let me know what I can do to help you." Well, Jermaine M. Davis is the kind of person who will take you up on your words and offers, so I delegated various jobs to each person. Soon I realized that their level of commitment and motivation dwindled rather quickly.

At the time of my break-though idea, I was engulfed in a very busy and intense speaking and teaching schedule. It was midterm time in the semester. I had ninety, twelve- to fifteen-page papers to grade, bi-monthly seminar classes to facilitate on campus for faculty members, and fifteen speeches to give in nineteen days, and I was also working on this book, which meant I had deadlines to meet. After I took my family and friends up on their offers to help with my break-through idea, I personally could not fully commit to the project for about five weeks. However, weekly I checked on their progress, and I found myself becoming annoyed, irritated, and frustrated when no one had made any substantial progress on their commitments. They were initially excited and enthusiastic, but their excitement came to an abrupt end. It was short lived. That's when it really hit me—this was my dream, my goal, and I must admit, I was a little discouraged. I had to be completely honest with myself and accept the fact that no one would ever be as hungry and as thirsty as I would be for and towards my dreams, goals, and aspirations. True motivation is inspired from within, but I believe most people are easily motivated by external influences. Initially, it was difficult for me to understand why my friends and family members gave up on such a great idea, but now I understand plainly; it was my goal and not their goal. They saw personal benefits for Jermaine M. Davis, but they didn't see benefits for themselves.

## The W.I.F.M. Theory

I truly believe that a great deal of human motivation can be directly connected to the *W.I.I.F.M. Theory:*

*W.I.I.F.M.* is an acronym that stands for "What's In It For Me?" People always want to know, "If I do this or that for you, how am I going to benefit?" People consistently and constantly want to know—What's In It For Me?

Guess what? I support this attitude when it comes to making your dreams, goals, and aspirations happen. *You* must be egotistical when striving for *your* goals just as *I* must be egotistical when striving for *my* goals.

When I say you should be egotistical in achieving your goals, I do not mean that you should be so selfish, self-centered, or so conceited that you exclude, offend, and disregard others. I simply mean looking out for Number One, which is you, my friend. I mean staying focused on your goals to get what you want and not allowing anyone to stand between you and your dreams. I mean thinking about *you* for a change, thinking about what makes you happy, what makes you smile, what makes your heart sing songs of praise, and what matters most to you as an individual.

## Benefits are our motivators

We are motivated because we want to fulfill a certain need, want, or desire. The higher the level of our need, want, or desire, the higher our level of motivation to fulfill our goals becomes. I believe that if you can identify the benefits in each of your goals, these benefits will serve as motivators during the intense trials and tribulations that you will surely face. I highly encourage you to be egotistical in setting and achieving your goals by always asking yourself, "What's in it for me?"

## Five additional questions you should ask yourself:

1. Why do I want to achieve this goal?
2. Why do I need to achieve this goal?
3. How will I benefit from achieving this goal?
4. What will achieving this goal do for my personal and professional, and spiritual life?
5. Will achieving this goal help me to become more effective, efficient, and productive in life, school, & work?

# How to apply the 8 steps
## A True Story

Atté Ontario had been the same height and weight since her third year of high school: 5 feet 6 inches and 150 pounds. Atté had been actively involved in sports throughout her high school and college career. Participating in school sports had been her secret to maintaining a weight of 150 pounds. Periodically, Atté jokingly commented about how she could stand to lose a few pounds here and there, but she was extremely comfortable with her weight and body size. Atté recently completed a triple Masters in Creative Writing, Marketing Communications, and Public Relations. She married her college sweetheart two years after graduating, and they had their first daughter, Nia Simone, after two years of being married.

During the pregnancy, Atté gained an extra thirty-five pounds, bringing her total weight gain to 185 pounds. She didn't think very much about the extra thirty-five pounds because she believed the extra weight would be lost post-pregnancy, twelve-weeks after giving birth (plus she had always been active in sports). However, a year after giving birth, Atté's post pregnancy weight is still 185 pounds, and she painfully acknowledges that she doesn't have that flat, perfect, and chiseled six-pack abdomen she once had. Atté is experiencing a plethora of negative thoughts and emotions, such as fear, self-doubt, resentment, anger, insecurity, irritation, and feelings of unattractiveness.

In her desperation and frustration, she tries a string of unsuccessful yo-yo diets. She goes to a local bookstore to read more about name brand weight loss programs as Slim Fast, Weight Watchers, Slimming World, Richard Simmons, Jenny Craig, The Okinawa Diet, The South Beach Diet, and of course, The Atkins Diet. Atté doesn't dismiss any of their suggestions and philosophies, but she becomes so overwhelmed and confused that she leaves the bookstore feeling helpless and hopeless. Next she experiences a mild case of depression, which causes her to snack throughout the day, and of course, she does not watch her caloric intake.

After seven months of an "I-don't-care" attitude, she gains another thirteen pounds, bringing her total weight gain to 198 pounds: the most she has ever weighed in her entire life. When she's around family and friends, she describes and refers to herself as little Miss Piggy, Tons of Fun, and Beer Gut Girl. It is obvious that her self-concept has changed drastically for the worse.

After a year and a half of weighing 198 pounds, Atté wakes up one morning, looks into the mirror, and says to herself, "I'm gross, and this is ridiculous. I've got to do something about this excessive weight. I want to get back to my 150 pounds. I need to lose forty-eight pounds, and my goal is to do it in six months. Atté doesn't know how to get started, but her best friend suggests that she follow the eight Steps to Success listed in Jermaine Davis' book *Get Up Off Your BUTT & Do It NOW!* Atté is determined to lose the unwanted forty-eight pounds, so she reads the entire book twice and reads the section on steps to success four times to make sure she understands the ideologies that Jermaine Davis is suggesting and encouraging. Atté designs a personal weight loss program strategy around each of the eight steps.

### Step 1: Clearly Identify What You Want and Know Why

Atté has clearly and specifically identified where she needs to focus her time, energy, and motivation. Her goal is to lose forty-eight pounds to get back to her desired weight of 150 pounds, and she wants to get her six-pack back and eliminate her beer gut as she calls it (she definitely does not like the mid-section area of her body). Atté's two main reasons for losing weight and toning up her stomach are to help her develop a positive self-image of herself and to improve her long-term physical health. She wants to feel good about herself when she looks into the mirror, and she wants to pass the value of goal setting and goal achieving along to her daughter, Nia Simone. After reading an article written by Dr. Thomas Fahey and Steve Blechman in the magazine *Fitness Rx*, Atté now understands that losing excessive fat in the abdomen area is more important than she thought for preventing future physical health problems. Dr. Fahey and Mr. Blechman state, "Ab cavity fat is dangerous because it is easily mobilized and can flood the liver and blood with dangerous fat. Cutting Ab fat helps fight the metabolic syndrome and reduces the risk of heart attack, cancer, and stroke. Also, many people store fat around their middles, which makes it difficult to show off well-toned muscles."

### Step 2: Perform a Needs Analysis: Knowledge, Skills, Desires, and Will

For Atté to successfully lose her forty-eight pounds and tone up her abdomen area, she must take a personal inventory of what she currently knows or will need to know regarding the most effective ways to tone her body and shed unwanted pounds in order to accomplish her goal. This means there is homework to be done before she starts to pursue this particular goal.

**Knowledge:** She must learn as much information as she can about various types of exercise programs to help her lose the forty-eight pounds and to tone up her stomach area. Atté must learn what kinds of healthy foods to eat and what kinds of unhealthy foods to avoid. She must discover what liquids and drinks are beneficial and which are liabilities in regards to her new lifestyle change.

**Skill:** Atté must learn which types of exercises will help her shed her unwanted pounds and which exercise machines will help her eliminate excess fat and tone up her abdominal area. For example, if she want to do Ab exercises, should she do Roman chair leg raises, hanging leg raises, bicycle maneuvers, vertical crunches, reverse crunches, exercise ball crunches, or side crunches? Atté must become competent and familiar with various exercise machines, strategies, and techniques in order to achieve her goals.

**Desires** (emotional state): Atté must make a conscious decision that she wants to accomplish this goal **NO MATTER WHAT.** She must emotionally prepare herself to maintain her exercise program and daily routine EVEN when she doesn't see immediate results after eating healthy and exercising regularly. Atté must understand that she does not have to FEEL like working out in order to work out because our feelings can be extremely misleading at times. Her challenge will be to discipline her emotions to follow pursuit, even when her emotions tell her to just give up and quit. She must learn to keep on keeping on when she is having feelings of self-doubt and when she feels like giving up and quitting her routine workout plan and healthy eating habits.

**Will** (mental state): This is where Atté must psychologically prepare herself for the mental challenges that lie before her, such as disbelief, uncertainty, the "just the way I am" attitude, and an "I-can't-do-it" mentality. Mental stamina, tenacity, and fortitude are all key tools to have in our mental toolbox when working on our dreams, goals, and aspirations. This is where practicing positive self-talk is key because Atté must tell herself over and over again that she is ready, willing, and able to persevere, no matter what mental roadblocks lie ahead of her. When she is shopping in the grocery store, she must be mentally strong enough to say no and to avoid buying certain foods or treats that will cause her to stray away from her goals. When she is at company outings or family functions, she must have the mental courage to say no to certain dinner choices and desserts. Since Atté knows she's an emotional eater, which means she eats and snacks based on her mood and emotional state, she must be mentally strong enough to say no to her favorite food dishes and desserts.

### Step 3: Write Down All Barriers and Obstacles

Atté must be truthful and honest about what potential barriers and obstacles might cause her to relapse or stray away. Once she has identified her barriers and obstacles, she must develop a defensive strategy to overcome her personal challenges. She identifies that one of her biggest barriers or obstacles is that when she's bored, she loves to snack on chocolate, cookies, and potato chips. This is more of a challenge for her because her spouse and daughter, Nia Simone, enjoy engaging in junk food eating quite regularly. This is a great temptation for Atté because the snack food cabinet is centrally located in the kitchen area of her home where she spends time preparing meals for her family. Atté has admitted that since she can remember, she has always worn her heart on her sleeve. In other words, she is a very emotional person (which is neither bad nor good), but Atté allows her emotional state to determine and dictate what she does on a daily basis. So if she doesn't FEEL like exercising, working out, and eating properly, then she probably won't stick to her goals.

If Atté is going to lose the forty-eight pounds and tone up her stomach area, she must develop a strategy to overcome these barriers and obstacles before they present themselves.

### Step 4: Develop a Dream Team

Simply, Atté must surround herself with like-minded people for strength, support, encouragement, and accountability reasons. She may decide to join a support group where the group members exercise together or give friendly and encouraging telephone calls to one another. Since she is in a household where she is the only one on a lifestyle change program, she must ask her loved ones to hold her accountable and be respectful and supportive of her new lifestyle change program. I refer to supportive friends and family as your Dream Team, and Dr. Phil refers to them as your "social support." I believe Dr. Phil does a really good job of reinforcing my main thoughts in his book *The Ultimate Weight Solution: The 7 Keys to Weight Loss Freedom* when he says, "Weight loss is not a do-it-yourself deal. If you expect to lose weight and keep it off, you must build and nurture relationships that affirm and uplift you in life-changing ways. Support from people you trust will flow through you like a current, energizing you to get results and have what you want. There is strength and power in support."

### Step 5: Ideas+Paper+A Pen= Written Goals

Now that Atté has determined what food and drink menus and exercise programs she must follow on a regular basis to help her accomplish her goals, it is imperative for her to write her daily and weekly goals down on paper. She should devise a plan on paper of what exercises she needs to perform daily, every other day, or whatever time she decides is suitable for her lifestyle and schedule. She should also write down what kinds of foods she should eat everyday in order to help her accomplish her goals. She needs a detailed plan on paper to review daily and weekly. She should also keep and maintain a daily log to keep track of her progress.

### Steps 6 and 7: Create a Roadmap for Directions and Deadlines = Maximum Productivity

Now Atté must develop a daily and weekly step-by-step plan for what she needs to do on a daily basis. She must decide what exercises to do on Monday, Wednesday, and Friday; what foods to prepare and eat for breakfast, lunch, and dinner; and she must decide how much weight to lose weekly and monthly to help her reach her goal of losing forty-eight unwanted pounds. Atté stated that she wants to lose forty-eight pounds at the end of six months. This means she must lose eight pounds per month, or two pounds per week, in order to achieve her goal in six months, which is her deadline. Having this monthly deadline and responsibility will help Atté effectively monitor and measure her progress. She may decide to check her weight every Wednesday to determine if she is meeting her goal of losing two pounds per week. If she is losing weight according to her weekly and monthly deadline, she should proceed with the game plan she has mapped out for herself. If she is not achieving her desired results when she monitors and measures her progress, Atté must reassess and decide what types of foods, drinks, or exercise programs she will need to start or stop to help her continue to lose her weight of two pounds per week.

I strongly suggest that all goals be broken down into smaller increments because they are more manageable and attainable in smaller increments than they are in larger increments. It is important that you gradually implement lifestyle changes that match your lifestyle and not the lifestyle others think you should have. If Atté wanted to be more specific, she could break the goal down into losing one pound per every three and a half days for the next six months. Atté is determined to lose two pounds per week and to do the necessary Ab exercises on a weekly basis in order to lose the total forty-eight pounds and to tone up her stomach area. The daily and weekly plan that Atté follows consistently will be the roadmap to take her to her desired destination, which is to have a toned stomach and to weigh 150 pounds again as she did in high school and college.

### Step 8: Be Egotistical

Yes, I believe if Atté is going to achieve her goal, she must be selfishly focused on her desired results, which are a toned stomach and a body weight of 150 pounds. Atté must prioritize regular and intentional exercise routines and healthy and proper eating choices into her new lifestyle. She will never be able to get that gorgeous six-pack stomach again or maintain her desired weight of 150 pounds for a lifetime unless she prioritizes her new values of eating healthy and exercising regularly. Bottom line: This is what it takes, and she must be selfish and stubborn about making this goal happen and making it a new habit. Although she's identified her Dream Team to help her succeed, she must keep in mind that this is HER goal and HER goal only. She must understand that no one is going to care about her goal more than she does. Atté must become "me focused" and "goal focused" until she achieves her goal. She must never allow anyone or anything to intercept or interfere with her personal goal.

# Final Thoughts

I have just shared with you some of the most effective tools and strategies I use in my life to help me achieve the things I truly want. I have also shared with you research from other successful people. And, believe it or not, I have also shared with you stories of unsuccessful people.

As I conclude *Get Off Your Butt & DO It NOW! Staying Motivated Even When You Don't FEEL Like IT*, I would like to say thank you for supporting this project and investing in your future endeavors.

Please study and master and not just read the tips, techniques, and strategies offered in this book. I encourage you to teach these concepts to colleagues, family members, and friends. According to Dr. Stephen Covey, you reinforce your learning when you teach others. He states, "When you teach once, you learn twice."

If you've read this book all the way through, congratulations! This kind of discipline and behavior communicates commitment and dedication. Remember there are no authentic get rich quick schemes or short cuts on the road to success. Paying your dues is a success principle and a law of nature that must be obeyed to achieve true greatness. Always keep in mind when things go wrong as they sometimes will—NEVER QUIT and NEVER GIVE UP!

*So please, please* apply these concepts to your life, and you will hear from Jermaine M. Davis in my next book. Thank you.

# About the Author

**Jermaine M. Davis** is a highly requested speaker working with colleges, corporations, and government and social service agencies across the United States.

Jermaine is an entrepreneur where he is C.E.O. & President of two companies, Seminars & Workshops, Inc. and Snack Attack Vending of Minnesota, Inc. He has been recognized as an excellent college instructor when he was presented with the prestigious Quality Instructor award by Student Support Services from a college within the Minnesota State Colleges & Universities School System.

Life wasn't always good for Jermaine Davis. Growing up in Chicago's inner city housing projects and coming from a single-parent family, Jermaine was determined to leave his poor, crime-ridden, and drug and gang infested neighborhood. After losing five family members and countless friends to street violence, he began studying success principles to apply to his own life and the lives of others. Jermaine was the first person in his family to graduate from college and to start his own business.

Jermaine is a full-time faculty member of speech communication at Century College in Minnesota. He has taught at University of Minnesota, University of Wisconsin-Superior, Lake Superior College, Brown College, Hennepin Technical College, and North Hennepin Community College. He has a solid management, marketing, and sales background with such companies as FRITO-LAY, INC. and KEEBLER COMPANY. Jermaine received his B.A. in Speech Communication from Elmhurst College, his M.A. in Speech Communication from the University of Wisconsin-Superior, and his M.Ed. in Teaching & Learning from Saint Mary's University. He also volunteers for women's shelters and men's programs in the Twin Cities, offering workshops on communication, assertiveness, motivation, self-esteem, and emotional control & anger management.

# A Special Invitation from the Author

If you are interested in bringing Jermaine M. Davis to your company, organization, or school for a conference, workshop, or book signing, please contact our corporate office at (651) 487-7576 or e-mail us at *jermaine@jermainedavis.com*. To learn more about products, other available workshops, and discounts on orders of 10 or more copies of *Get Up Off Your Butt & Do It NOW!*, please call, e-mail us, or visit our website at www.jermainedavis.com.

To find out about our discount program for resellers of *Get Up Off Your Butt & Do It NOW!*, please contact our Special sales department at (651) 487-7576 or (773) 936-0222.

### Here are the best ways Jermaine can help your organization:
- Keynote and Endnote Presentations
- Full-and Multi-Day Residencies
- New Employee and Student Orientation
- Faculty and Professional Staff Development Programs
- Professional Association Conferences
- Parents' Day Programs
- Student Leadership and Team Building Training
- Diversity and Multi-cultural Programs
- Minority Student Programs
- Martin Luther King and Black History Month Celebrations
- Greek Life: Fraternities and Sororities Programs
- Graduation Keynotes
- High School Conferences
- Religious and Spiritual Conferences and Retreats
- Parent Teacher Association Meetings